THE ADVENTURES OF A SLAVE GIRL

Edinburgh Studies on the Ottoman Empire
Series Editor: Kent F. Schull

Published and forthcoming titles

The Ottoman Ulema and the Quest for an Islamic Constitution
Yakoob Ahmed

Sufism and Power in the Ottoman Empire
Kameliya N. Atanasova

The Ottoman Canon and the Construction of Arabic and Turkish Literatures
C. Ceyhun Arslan

Migrating Texts
Edited by Marilyn Booth

Ottoman Translations
Edited by Marilyn Booth and Claire Savina

Death and Life in the Ottoman Palace
Douglas Scott Brookes

Conscripting Breadwinner Soldiers in the Late Ottoman Empire
Kate Dannies

Corruption in the Ottoman Polity
Edited by Bogaç A. Ergene and Cengiz Kirli

Ottoman Sunnism
Edited by Vefa Erginbaş

Ethnic Cleansing in Western Anatolia, 1912–1923
Umit Eser

Jews and Palestinians in the Late Ottoman Era, 1908–1914
Louis A. Fishman

Governing Migration in the Late Ottoman Empire
Ella Fratantuono

Spiritual Vernacular of the Early Ottoman Frontier
Carlos Grenier

The Politics of Armenian Migration to North America, 1885–1915
David Gutman

The Kizilbash-Alevis in Ottoman Anatolia
Ayfer Karakaya-Stump

Çemberlitaş Hamami in Istanbul
Nina Macaraig

Hagia Sophia in the Long Nineteenth Century
Edited by Emily Neumeier and Benjamin Anderson

The Kurdish Nobility in the Ottoman Empire
Nilay Özok-Gündoğan

Armenians and Land Disputes in the Ottoman Empire, 1850–1914
Mehmet Polatel

Nineteenth-Century Local Governance in Ottoman Bulgaria
Safa Saraçoğlu

Prisons in the Late Ottoman Empire
Kent F. Schull

The Adventures of a Slave Girl
Samipaşazade Sezai, translated from the Ottoman Turkish original, edited and introduced by Burcu Karahan and İclal Vanwesenbeeck

The Architecture of Bibliophilia
Yavuz Sezer

Biography of an Ottoman Provincial Town
Ali Sipahi

Ruler Visibility and Popular Belonging in the Ottoman Empire
Darin Stephanov

Managing Religious Diversity in the Ottoman Empire
Masayuki Ueno

The North Caucasus Borderland
Murat Yaşar

Children and Childhood in the Ottoman Empire
Edited by Gülay Yılmaz and Fruma Zachs

edinburghuniversitypress.com/series/esoe

THE ADVENTURES OF A SLAVE GIRL

AN OTTOMAN NOVEL BY SAMİPAŞAZADE SEZAİ

Translated from the Ottoman Turkish original,
edited and introduced by
Burcu Karahan and İclal Vanwesenbeeck

EDINBURGH
University Press

Edinburgh University Press is one of the leading university presses in the UK. Publishing new research in the arts and humanities, EUP connects people and ideas to inspire creative thinking, open new perspectives and shape the world we live in. For more information, visit www.edinburghuniversitypress.com.

Cover image: © Ali Yaycıoğlu
Cover design: Stuart Dalziel

Edinburgh University Press Ltd
13 Infirmary Street, Edinburgh EH1 1LT

Typeset in Jaghbuni by
Cheshire Typesetting Ltd, Cuddington, Cheshire
Printed and bound in the UK using 100% renewable electricity by
CPI Group (UK) Ltd

A CIP record for this book is available from the British Library

ISBN 978 1 3995 5854 9 (hardback)
ISBN 978 1 3995 5855 6 (paperback)
ISBN 978 1 3995 5857 0 (webready PDF)
ISBN 978 1 3995 5856 3 (epub)

Contents

Figures

Acknowledgements

The preparation of *The Adventures of a Slave Girl* was a journey both joyful and demanding, made possible by the support and generosity of many colleagues. We are profoundly grateful to all who shared their time, insight and encouragement along the way.

When we had only a single translated chapter, we reached out to Ehud Toledano for his thoughts on the text and our approach. Since he is a leading scholar on Ottoman slavery and was the first to frame Sezai's novel within that discourse, his critical feedback and enthusiastic encouragement were foundational to our efforts.

The turning point for this project was no doubt our meeting with Kent Schull, to whom we owe lasting thanks. He believed in the project, helped us envision it as a scholarly publication and guided its development with generosity.

We are also indebted to the members of the Edinburgh University Press's Ottoman Empire Series Advisory Board, to the anonymous reviewers for their suggestions and support of this project and to our editor, Rachel Bridgewater, whose professionalism helped bring this work to light.

It is Ceyda Karamürsel's foreword that positions this literary translation in a historical context, especially concerning female slavery in the late Ottoman Empire. For this critical foreword and for her generous help with our chronology, we would like to express our profound gratitude and indebtedness to her.

We are truly grateful for our work to be crowned by our dear friend Ali Yaycıoğlu's beautiful cover art.

Throughout the process, we benefited from the careful eyes and thoughtful feedback of many friends and colleagues, including Aslı Gür, Kelda Jamison, Randy Richardson, A. J. Naddaff and Özgül Özdemir, who read parts of the translation at various stages. Patricia Blessing guided us through some of the artwork; Denise Gill deepened our understanding of the call to prayer in mid-nineteenth-century Istanbul, and Vladimir Hamed-Troyansky helped us with the chronology. Our sincere thanks go to Yunus Emre Şebin as well, for transcribing the slave sale contracts from the nineteenth-century Ottoman Empire.

Given the visual richness of Sezai's novel, we were especially committed to capturing the world it evokes. We thank Zeki Aslan at the Istanbul Municipality Atatürk Library (IBB Atatürk Kitaplığı), for his help; archivists Nebahat Yusoğlu and Ata Yersu at the Aşiyan Museum Archives, for their assistance; Ömer Erdem from Kapı Yayınları, for generously sharing with us the 1924 photograph of Sezai at Cemal Mithat Kuntay's apartment; and the Gennadius Librarians at the American School of Classical Studies at Athens (ASCSA), the National Portrait Gallery and Musée des Augustins, Ville de Toulouse. A special thank you to Emma Gordon at Sotheby's UK, for facilitating the inclusion of Jean-Léon Gérôme's *Jeune fille du Caire* in the translation. Finally, we are grateful to our families. We come from multi-lingual households, and as we translated *The Adventures of a Slave Girl* on two separate coasts, over a span of three years, Aaron, Atlas, Ayla, Birger and Doğa's patience, comments, way with words and sense of humour sustained us through the long hours of transcription and translation. They became, inevitably, part of this work.

Translators' Note

The Adventures of a Slave Girl was originally written in Ottoman Turkish using the Perso-Arabic script. The novel was published in 1888, during the Hamidian era, and then again in 1924, under the newly established Turkish republic. While we conducted a comparative reading of both editions, this translation is based on the 1924 Ottoman Turkish edition of the novel.

In 1928, modern Turkey adopted the Latin alphabet, thereby ending the use of Ottoman Turkish in print. While there is a lexical legacy of Ottoman Turkish in today's modern Turkish, the relationship remains an uneasy one, perhaps best seen in the modern transcriptions of various Ottoman novels in Turkish. This poses a particular challenge for translators of Ottoman Turkish because, even though Ottoman Turkish is closely related to modern Turkish, it is, by conservative measures, a dead language and cannot be fully understood or interpreted simply by knowing modern Turkish. Aware of the linguistic distance between us and the Ottoman language in the novel, we engaged in endless negotiations and hermeneutical efforts; at times, we relied on our literary imagination for semantic clues. Translating this novel also required us to silence our modern Turkish and our acquired ways of reading modern novels and, instead, tune into the idiosyncratic ethos of the Ottoman novel with its unique rhythm, artistic ambitions and structural nuances.

We paid particular attention to retaining the long sentence structures, elaborate adjective constructions and seemingly superfluous but artistically idiosyncratic *izafe*.[1] We were also mindful of Sezai's aspiration to

[1] In the Ottoman language, influences from Arabic and Persian were not limited to vocabulary but also extended to grammatical structures. Various constructions from these languages, which are entirely alien to Turkish, became notably prevalent. Among these is the Persian *izafe*, a grammatical particle meaning 'addition'. This particle connects the head of a noun phrase to the modifying noun or adjective that follows it, integrating non-Turkish syntactic elements into the Ottoman linguistic framework.

describe characters and landscapes with a rich and endearing vocabulary. For Sezai, the detailed description of the elderly woman's hair in Chapter Two, of the home of the slave trader in Chapter Four, or the intricate portrayal of the tiles in the wealthy merchant's mansion in Egypt are not deviations or mere embellishments but stylistic experiments with character development and setting. To preserve what we consider the authentic ethos of the Ottoman novel, we calibrated our translation to align with Sezai's own artistic choices and sensibilities.

Staying true to the original text was a priority for us; however, we took a liberal approach with the translation of the title. The original title, *Sergüzeşt*, means 'adventure' in Persian. We believe that Sezai's choice of a common and non-specific noun may have been a deliberate act of evasion, particularly to bypass the heavy censorship of Abdülhamid II. The original title veils rather than reveals the anti-slavery storyline, yet we know from Sezai's 1924 introduction that he does not treat the concept of 'adventure' neutrally but instead connects it intricately to Dilber's experiences as an enslaved girl and her ordeals in the pursuit of freedom. Therefore, we decided to keep the core term 'adventure' in the English title, but framed it within the context of slavery, in line with Sezai's introduction, narrative plot and writerly sensibilities.

Our addition of the subtitle, 'an Ottoman novel', was intended to highlight the novel's distinct literary framework rather than a political decision. As translators, we believe that there are certain stylistic threads that characterise Ottoman novels written between 1880 and 1908, setting them apart from a broadly defined Turkish literary tradition. This distinction is crucial for appreciating the novel within its historical and cultural milieu; thus, we felt it essential to reflect its Ottoman literary heritage in the title.

One such unique cultural detail in the novel is the notation of time. The Ottoman Empire used the Islamic calendar and a sunrise-to-sunset hour system. In this translation, we retained the original temporal references without converting them to western time conventions or the Gregorian calendar, ensuring that the historical framework of the novel remains intact. However, we provided footnotes to clarify these temporal references for the reader.

Another point of peculiarity in the novel is Sezai's persistent use of numeric ranges instead of specific figures when referring to people's ages, days, or measurements. We preserved these ranges only when they were critical to the narrative; in other instances, we opted for the lower number to maintain clarity and readability. A similar approach guided our decision to leave certain culturally specific words untranslated. By doing so, we aimed to allow readers to engage more deeply with the text and immerse themselves in its unique lexical space.

As opposed to temporal conversions and the translation of culture-specific terms, disentangling Sezai's syntax and grammar posed significant challenges. His penchant for paragraph-long sentences, often weaving together multiple simultaneous actions, compelled us to streamline syntax while preserving lexical and stylistic richness. Where we detected a clear causal relationship, we broke down lengthy sentences for temporal clarity. However, in instances of deliberate semantic ambiguity, we chose to preserve it for artistic reasons.

As we transcribed the Ottoman text, we often found ourselves in intense proximity to what was, at times, a protean work. We were frequently perplexed by our previous readings of certain passages, questioning whether the textual enigmas were intentional or the result of a vowel shift, a misprint, orthographic mistakes, or syntactical and morphological ambiguities. Any late-nineteenth-century Ottoman text poses similar challenges, with inherent mysteries and shifting meanings that can render the novel elusive. For us, this aspect was simultaneously challenging, liberating and anxiety-inducing. Fortunately, we had the advantage of being co-translators. This project reaffirmed the benefits of co-translation, particularly in Ottoman literature. Our shared principles of trust and open-mindedness, combined with our love of Late Ottoman literature, allowed us to work efficiently. We went over every word, sentence and chapter together – questioning lexical possibilities, ensuring accuracy and negotiating the meanings behind what we consider to be unapologetically obscure passages in Ottoman.

Despite its challenges, working on Sezai's novel also brought us profound joy. We immersed ourselves in the world of the 1880s Ottoman Empire, imagining its literary circles, painting scenes inspired by the novel and envisioning the waters of the Sea of Marmara at sunrise and sunset, through both Sezai's meticulous descriptions and Celal's orientalist gaze. We spent hours in the archives tracing artistic and historical references, listening to the songs mentioned in the novel and uncovering the cultural nuances embedded in its pages. This deep dive into Sezai's novel, its era and its culture not only enriched our translation process but also delightfully transformed our lives. For this transformative experience, we thank Sezai Bey from the bottom of our hearts.

Burcu Karahan and İclal Vanwesenbeeck

Foreword

Ceyda Karamürsel

Few historical comparisons have proven as persistently difficult – or as politically charged – as placing the plantation and chattel slavery of the Americas side by side with other forms of enslavement across the globe. The reasons for this difficulty are many. On the one hand lies the anomalous nature of American or Atlantic chattel slavery itself, which, unlike most practices in other parts of the world, defined enslaved people purely in proprietary terms – an anomaly that strikes us as distinct even within the millennia-long horror of human bondage across societies.[1] On the other hand, we are shaped by our own scholarly orientations: the economic and labour-centred frameworks through which we have come to understand American slavery tend to obscure other registers, particularly those less legible in quantitative or transactional terms.[2] More significantly perhaps, the still-unresolved and politically urgent question of race in the Atlantic world in general and in the United States in particular compels us, for good reason, to think in stark contrasts, often in plain black and white. That moral clarity, while essential, has also rendered certain comparative gestures fraught. As a result, it is not only difficult but also often politically undesirable to trace parallels that may appear to flatten the singular violence of racialised slavery in the Americas.[3]

[1] Gross, *Double Character*.

[2] See, for example, Beckert, *Empire of Cotton*; Baptist, *The Half Has Never Been Told*; Rosenthal, *Accounting for Slavery*; Johnson, *River of Dark Dreams*, which have productively re-centred American slavery within histories of capitalism, labour and accumulation, while also privileging forms of analysis most legible in economic, quantitative and transactional terms.

[3] On the ethical and political stakes that render comparison difficult and undesirable in the study of Atlantic racial slavery, see especially Hartman, *Lose Your Mother*.

This difficulty is further compounded by the sheer asymmetry of the historical record. The exceptional documentation of American or Atlantic slavery – its paper trails, narratives, plantation ledgers, court proceedings and autobiographies – perhaps precisely because it was such 'big business', stands in marked contrast to the relative archival silence that characterises most other forms of enslavement, particularly in the Ottoman, Indian Ocean and even Mediterranean worlds.[4] That disparity in existing documentation, traced in the Ottoman case almost entirely through the state archive, has shaped not only what we know, but also how we come to know it, and, more crucially, what we are able or willing to place in a comparative frame. Consequently, our understanding of these different modalities of extreme exploitation remains uneven, and our capacity to place them in meaningful conversation with one another remains, at best, incomplete.

The Adventures of a Slave Girl: An Ottoman Novel offers a valuable point of entry for reckoning with the frictions of connection and comparison that shape the study of slavery's global histories: distortions born of mismatched vocabularies of law, lawlessness, race and violence; of interpretive conventions that determine what counts as legible evidence and what does not; and of the uneven archival depth that continues to delimit our understanding of slavery's layered contexts. As the first English translation of what is widely regarded as the first – and in some ways only – abolitionist novel to emerge from the nineteenth-century Ottoman context, it provides a close, if at times problematic, window onto Ottoman slavery, authored by someone who was not only a witness to the institution but also, however reluctantly, a participant in its perpetuation. While fictional in form, the account is grounded in the author Samipaşazade Sezai's own experience of the practices of elite households, especially his own. As the translators detail in the volume's introduction, like many of his contemporaries of similar social and economic background, Sezai was born to a formerly enslaved mother and raised in an affluent household shaped by the presence and labour of enslaved people, circumstances that gave him an intimate and complex understanding of the institution.[5] While his words – as those of a slaveholder – demand a critical reading, the novel nevertheless offers a rare opportunity to bring into comparative view literary takes on slavery shaped by diverse social, political, legal and economic conditions across the globe.

[4] For two excellent examples of the documentary density of Atlantic and American slavery, see Scott, *Freedom Papers*; McDaniel, *Sweet Taste of Liberty*.

[5] Toledano, 'Late Ottoman Concepts of Slavery'.

Throughout the narrative of *The Adventures of a Slave Girl*, we glimpse not only the commercial structures and rhythms of the Ottoman slave trade, the workings of its markets, its financial aspects and domestic arrangements, but also its multi-racial, multi-ethnic, multi-lingual, gendered and deeply intimate composition. Written in a distinctly emotional tone, intended to stir the reader's moral imagination and inspire action – if not in public, then at least in private – the novel offers striking detail. As the translators also note in the introduction, for one, geography's complicity in the matter is well established throughout the book. Places such as the neighbourhood of Tophane in Istanbul or the River Nile in Egypt emerge not as neutral settings but almost as villainous characters in their own right, integral to the architecture of slavery and the slave trade. Elite households across the expanse of the empire appear as both consumers and reproducers of enslaved labour, while the enslaved themselves are rendered in close and often painful detail, undergoing processes of discipline and training that reveal the intimate and structural violences embedded in domestic slavery.

Beyond providing a well-informed insider's view into the mechanisms and particularities of Ottoman slavery, *The Adventures of a Slave Girl*'s real value lies in the connective horizon it opens up: the contested meanings of freedom and the imagined shape of life – or its very impossibility – for those emerging from bondage.[6] Like many of its counterparts elsewhere, especially in the Americas, the novel speaks of slavery and its injustices, not merely to expose them, but in order to articulate a vision of a more equal, just and free society.[7] In other words, its ultimate concern is not solely or necessarily slavery itself, but what might come after it. The volume's contribution to the broader literature on slavery and abolition, then, lies not only in the flawed yet revealing depiction of the institution of slavery and slave trade in the Ottoman Empire found in the novel, but in the invitation that the volume extends to think comparatively and relationally about freedom; to situate the Ottoman imagination of emancipation within a transforming global order; and to consider its legal, political, economic and moral implications across connected geographies.

This shift in focus from slavery to freedom carries, for both the late-nineteenth-century author and for us today, significant historiographical

[6] On emancipation as a contested and uneven process, rather than a clear endpoint, see Cooper, Holt and Scott, *Beyond Slavery*.

[7] For abolitionist literature and print culture as vehicles for articulating and connecting broader moral and political visions of equality and freedom, see Davis, *The Problem of Slavery in the Age of Emancipation*; Sinha, *The Slave's Cause*.

weight. If slavery presents enduring challenges to the historian through the frictions of comparison, freedom opens onto a different horizon: a shared, if unevenly expressed, dream of a better world, framed by the unmistakably alluring yet persistently elusive (over)promise of emancipation.[8] Perhaps it is this very abstraction – its fluidity and capacity to bend across contexts – that makes freedom a more hospitable terrain for relational and connective thinking, where slavery, dense with materiality and pain, so often resists it. Read against the grain and in conversation with the broader abolitionist literature, further discussed below, *The Adventures of a Slave Girl* becomes more than a reflection on Ottoman slavery: it offers a generative site for exploring what freedom has meant – and might still mean – across distinct yet entangled histories.

That a shared horizon of freedom exists and can serve as a basis for comparative and connective thinking must not, however, eclipse the different forms that abolitionism assumed across time and place, or the distinct historical conditions in which the struggle against slavery was imagined, mobilised and waged. Abolitionism was a battle fought simultaneously on multiple fronts, a fight that was not only geographically dispersed and historically contingent but also strategically diverse.[9] While these struggles were at times linked and even mutually shaped or invigorated by one another, the contours of abolition in North America differed markedly from those in the Caribbean, the African continent, Europe, or the Ottoman and Indian Ocean worlds. Each context demanded its own particular set of strategic articulations, giving distinct form and vocabulary to what we might broadly describe as global abolitionism. This multiplicity of fronts did not merely reflect regional variation. It also pointed to divergent definitions, claims, tactics, venues and channels of resistance.

For many, abolition was a practical struggle, waged through the slow, daily contestation of the mundane and often invisible mechanics of enslavement. It was in these everyday efforts – modest in scale but cumulative in effect – that much of the labour of abolition took place. As David Ruggles, an abolitionist and the founding member of the New York Committee of Vigilance, who famously aided Frederick Douglass's escape from slavery, insisted, it was just as vital to confront the 'minor evils' of slavery as it was to pursue the 'mighty revolution' of general abolition.[10] While Ruggles and others never abandoned the noble cause of total abolition, they underscored the importance of 'alleviating [the

[8] Foner, *The Story of American Freedom*, p. xiv.

[9] Sinha, *The Slave's Cause*.

[10] *First Annual Report of the New York Committee of Vigilance for the Year 1837*, p. 13.

enslaved people's] sufferings, affording them protection, giving them counsel, and thus in [their] individual spheres of action, prov[ing] [them] selves practical abolitionists'.[11] By the 1850s, especially in the wake of such legal developments as the Fugitive Slave Act of 1850, abolitionism in the United States inevitably took a more radical turn, and many activists came to view this practical mode of engagement, shaped by everyday urgencies and localised emergencies, as the only viable path toward achieving general abolition.[12] Abolitionist newspapers went so far as to denounce abstract or rhetorical commitments to abolition as empty gestures or, worse, as political opportunism.[13] For them, true abolitionism demanded action in the immediate, concrete realm of daily life: a politics of care, protection and intervention as much as one of principle and proclamation.

This dismissal, while rooted in the political atmosphere of antebellum America, carried a resonance that extended beyond the Atlantic world, including the Ottoman Empire, where abolitionist activity often came to unfold in piecemeal, concealed, subversive and necessarily local ways, exemplifying the uneven, fragmented and contextually rooted character of abolitionism worldwide.[14] That said, print culture, especially newspapers and serialised publications, remained a central channel through which both the horrors of slavery and anti-slavery ideas reached a broad audience. These venues were not merely sites for articulating moral critiques of slavery but more crucially served, as mentioned above, as platforms for debating broader political questions of citizenship and state-belonging. Fictional works such as Harriet Beecher Stowe's *Uncle Tom's Cabin*, which sold 300,000 copies within the year it was published, demonstrated the powerful affective and mobilising potential of narrative.[15] Other bestsellers, such as Frederick Douglass's *Narrative of the Life of Frederick Douglass, an American Slave* or Solomon Northup's *Twelve Years a Slave*, which offered first-hand testimonies of the institution, reached

[11] Ibid.

[12] Sinha, *The Slave's Cause*, pp. 405–6.

[13] For an illustrative example of the critique of abolitionism as 'a mere mock philanthropy, without soul, espoused for partisan purposes ... simply to elevate white demagogues to office', see 'Practical Abolitionism'.

[14] Karamursel, 'Fighting the Minor Evils', p. 618.

[15] Originally serialised in the weekly abolitionist newspaper *The National Era* in 1851–52, Harriet Beecher Stowe's novel *Uncle Tom's Cabin; or, Life among the Lowly* was published in book form in 1852 and quickly became an international bestseller, selling approximately two million copies worldwide by 1857.

wide audiences and deeply shaped public sentiment.[16] Whether fictional or testimonial, such texts helped tie the personal to the political, casting the struggle against slavery as a broader fight for justice, dignity and inclusion within and across national and transnational contexts.

While a late addition to the global archive of abolitionist literature, *The Adventures of a Slave Girl* is nonetheless a significant extension of a body of work that had long demonstrated its power in disseminating ideas and inspiring action. As discussed above, its value lies not only in its vivid depiction of Ottoman slavery but also in the connective horizon that it opens for exploring contested meanings of freedom and the imagined shape of social life and political order after slavery. The novel is at once familiar and distant: familiar in its narrative arc of captivity, resistance and the pursuit of freedom; distant in its geographic origins and historical context. This tension – between the known and the unfamiliar – makes the work all the more compelling, as both a narrative and an object of study, inviting readers from the English-speaking world to expand their conceptual and geographical frames of abolition beyond the Atlantic.

All in all, *The Adventures of a Slave Girl* unsettles the established geographies of anti-slavery struggle, opening a space for thinking across imperial, regional and linguistic divides. It sharpens our sense of how the fight against slavery unfolded in uneven, unlikely, locally-rooted and often piece-meal ways, reminding us that slavery's history was never confined to the Atlantic world, and neither was its contestation. At a moment when the comparative study of slavery and freedom remains both politically urgent and historiographically fraught, the novel offers a distinct vantage point: one that bridges the Atlantic and the Ottoman, the testimonial and the literary, the familiar and the distant. In doing so, it brings us closer to understanding not only the world that slavery made, but also the varied and sometimes contradictory traditions of anti-slavery thought and practice that arose in response. These traditions, whether radical or reformist, legal or literary, local or transnational, continue to provide us with conceptual tools to name and confront injustice. In this sense, *The Adventures of a Slave Girl* is more than a window into a particular past; it is a call to engage with the enduring afterlives of slavery in the present, and to think carefully and comparatively about the possibilities and limits of freedom – and the persistent labour it demands.

[16] Douglass, *Narrative of the Life of Frederick Douglass, an American Slave*; Northup, *Twelve Years a Slave*.

Works Cited

Baptist, Edward E. *The Half Has Never Been Told: Slavery and the Making of American Capitalism*. Basic Books, 2014.

Beckert, Sven. *Empire of Cotton: A Global History*. Alfred A. Knopf, 2014.

Beecher Stowe, Harriet. *Uncle Tom's Cabin; or, Life among the Lowly*. John P. Jewett & Company; Jewett, Proctor & Worthington, 1852.

Copper, Frederick, Thomas C. Holt and Rebecca J. Scott, *Beyond Slavery: Explorations of Race, Labor, and Citizenship in Postemancipation Societies*. University of North Carolina Press, 2000.

Davis, David Brion. *The Problem of Slavery in the Age of Emancipation*. Alfred A. Knopf, 2014.

Douglass, Frederick. *Narrative of the Life of Frederick Douglass, an American Slave*. Boston Anti-Slavery Office, 1845.

———. 'Practical Abolitionism'. *Frederick Douglass' Paper*, 15 June 1855.

First Annual Report of the New York Committee of Vigilance for the Year 1837: Together with Important Facts Relative to Their Proceedings. Piercy and Reed, 1837.

Foner, Eric. *The Story of American Freedom*. W. W. Norton & Company, 1998.

Gross, Ariela J. *Double Character: Slavery and Mastery in the Antebellum Southern Courtroom*. Princeton University Press, 2000.

Hartman, Saidiya. *Lose Your Mother: A Journey along the Atlantic Slave Route*. Farrar, Straus and Giroux, 2007.

Johnson, Walter. *River of Dark Dreams: Slavery and Empire in the Cotton Kingdom*. Harvard University Press, 2013.

Karamürsel, Ceyda. 'Fighting the Minor Evils: Slavery and the Diverse Lives of Abolitionism in the Ottoman Empire', *International Journal of Middle East Studies*, vol. 56, no. 4, 2025, pp. 610–26.

McDaniel, Caleb. *Sweet Taste of Liberty: A True Story of Slavery and Restitution in America*. Oxford University Press, 2019.

Northup, Solomon. *Twelve Years a Slave*. Derby and Miller, 1853.

Rosenthal, Caitlin. *Accounting for Slavery: Masters and Management*. Harvard University Press, 2018.

Scott, Rebecca J. *Freedom Papers: An Atlantic Odyssey in the Age of Emancipation*. Harvard University Press, 2012.

Sinha, Manisha. *The Slave's Cause: A History of Abolition*. Yale University Press, 2016.

Toledano, Ehud R. 'Late Ottoman Concepts of Slavery'. *Poetics Today*, vol. 14, no. 3, 1993, pp. 477–506.

Introduction: Samipaşazade Sezai and the Tanzimat

O face of freedom, how enchanting you are!
Though freed from bondage, we remain a slave to your love.

Namık Kemal, 'Ode to Freedom'

Samipaşazade Sezai was the son of a slave girl. His mother, Gülarayiş Hanım, like Dilber, the protagonist of his novel *The Adventures of a Slave Girl*, was brought from the Caucasus as a slave to the Ottoman imperial capital, Istanbul. Unlike his enslaved mother, his father, Abdurrahman Sami Pasha (1795–1878), had descended from a family of religious scholars and high-ranking statesmen from the Morea (Peloponnese) and served as the first Minister of Education (1857–61) in the Ottoman Empire.

Abdurrahman Sami Pasha had relocated his family to Cairo after the fall of Tripolitsa during the Greek War of Independence (1821–29). He worked for the governor of Egypt, Muhammad Ali Pasha, for twenty-five years in high-profile positions. When Muhammad Ali Pasha's son was succeeded by Abbas I, Abdurrahman Sami Pasha in 1849 moved his family again, this time to Istanbul.

Sezai was born in 1859, a decade after the family's move and during an era of sweeping political and social reforms that not only restructured the empire's educational, judicial and military institutions, but also redefined the discourse on freedom and justice. This period of western-inspired reform and modernisation, known as the Tanzimat (1839–76), aimed at centralising the Ottoman Empire, fundamentally shaping the cultural, intellectual and literary landscape. Initiated under Sultan Abdülmecid I (1839–61), the reforms were formalised through two landmark imperial edicts: the Noble Edict of the Rose Chamber (*Hatt-ı Şerif* of Gülhane) in 1839 and the Imperial Reform Edict of 1856 (*Hatt-ı Hümayun*), an Ottoman Bill of Rights, which introduced and reinforced guarantees of life, property and legal rights for all Ottoman subjects, regardless of religion. The promised equality, however, stopped short for the empire's enslaved subjects.

The challenge of reconciling Tanzimat reforms with the religious foundations of the empire and deeply rooted social traditions remained a persistent struggle throughout the Late Ottoman period. This tension created a duality within Ottoman society, where modernisation efforts coexisted with enduring older forms, and a new European way of life with imported clothes, furniture and music stores coexisted with the old one, thus leading to an era marked by both progress and resistance, a constant push and pull between change and tradition. In some cases, this duality was seen as the biggest obstacle to modernisation. It was for this reason that Ahmet Hamdi Tanpınar (1901–62), one of the most important writers and literary critics of the Republican era, described this duality – engrained in everyday language and intellectual discourse even today through the terms coined at that time, *alafranga* and *alaturka* – as 'the greatest fatality of the Tanzimat era'.[1]

Sezai grew up in an era marked by such contradictions and in a house that, in many ways, embodied and represented the quintessential duality of the Tanzimat. Abdurrahman Sami Pasha's *konak*, just like other mansions of high-ranking statesmen in nineteenth-century Istanbul, was not just a big multi-generational mansion run by numerous servants and enslaved individuals, but presented an Ottoman lifestyle where the *konak* owners – high-ranking statesmen, pashas and foreign ambassadors – frequently held musical, literary and political gatherings.[2] Abdurrahman Sami Pasha and his older son Abdüllatif Subhi Pasha (1818–86), who served as Ottoman Minister of Foundations, Education, and Treasury and Finance, lived in equally grand mansions, both of which were meeting places for the Tanzimat elite, where intellectual, literary and cultural exchanges took place and networks of patronage developed.[3] In her memoirs of her grandfather, Abdüllatif Subhi Pasha, Seniha Sami Moralı has recounted her grandfather's and her great-grandfather's mansions as follows:

> The *selamlık*[4] section of the mansion was like an academy visited by eastern and western scholars and literary figures. Scholars such as Renan[5] and

[1] Tanpınar, *19. Asır Türk Edebiyatı Tarihi*, p. 136.

[2] For more on *konak*s and Ottoman culture surrounding them, see Bertram, *Imagining The Turkish House*.

[3] Güven, *Sami Paşazade Sezayi ve Eserleri*, pp. 27–30.

[4] The section of an Ottoman house reserved for men.

[5] Ernest Renan (1823–92), French orientalist, philosopher, and historian.

> Mor[d]tmann[6] were hosted there. Mor[d]tmann stayed there for years and taught [Abdüllatif Subhi] Pasha's sons. As in the Sami Pasha mansion, guests came and stayed from the Ottoman provinces and foreign states such as India, Afghanistan and Iran.[7]

Abdurrahman Sami Pasha's mansion, frequented by prominent reform-minded intellectuals and writers of the time, such as Ziya Pasha, Ahmed Vefik Pasha, Ali Suavi, Osman Nevres, Yenişehirli Avni Bey and Üsküdarlı Hakkı Bey, was indeed a school for Sezai. He received his education there from these Tanzimat intellectuals. Some became his Arabic and Persian instructors, while others taught him French and German. Abdurrahman Sami Pasha himself gave lessons on history, philosophy, Rumi's *Masnavi* and Saadi's *Gulistan* to his own children and grandchildren.

One of the regulars of Sami Pasha's mansion was Monsieur Fabre, a Frenchman under the patronage of Sami Pasha, who became Sezai's French tutor. Sezai wrote that Fabre 'would present examples from the French Revolution to encourage us toward a national uprising'.[8] Sezai's nephew (Subhi Pasha's son) Ayetullah Bey was among the founders of the Young Ottomans, and later Sezai himself would join the Young Turks. Remembering his time in the mansions of the father and son and referring to reformist and revolutionary political ideas, Yenişehirli Avni wrote: 'The Young Turk movement was just beginning to emerge. In Sami and Subhi Pashas' mansions, which brought together prominent intellectuals in Istanbul from both the East and the West, these ideas were not only discussed but also actively supported and cultivated'.[9]

Sami Pasha's summer residence in Çamlıca also served as an intellectual enclave. In addition to his own children, he also tutored several neighbours' children, among them the famous poet and playwright Abdülhak Hamid Tarhan (1852–1937), who would later be called *şair-i azam* (the greatest poet). It was in this rarefied milieu that Sezai, still a young boy, first encountered Tarhan and Recaizade Mahmut Ekrem (1847–1914), who would also go on to become another seminal figure in later Tanzimat literature, advocating for the westernisation of Ottoman literature. These three young literary figures spent their summers in the neighbouring mansions and went on to become some of the most prominent writers of the late Tanzimat era, regarded as pillars of modern Turkish literature, each

[6] Andreas David Mordtmann (1811–79), German orientalist, diplomat, missionary, who lived in Ottoman Istanbul for thirty-five years.

[7] Moralı, 'Türk Kültürüne Büyük Hizmetleri Dokunan bir Devlet Adamı', pp. 69–74.

[8] Güven, *Sami Paşazade Sezayi ve Eserleri*, p. 32.

[9] Özgül, *Yenişehirli Avni*, p. 44.

contributing uniquely to its evolution. Sezai and Ekrem each wrote only one novel, *The Adventures of a Slave Girl* and *Araba Sevdası* (The Carriage Affair, 1896), respectively, both published within the same decade. Ten years after Ekrem's death, Sezai honoured his close friend by dedicating the second (1924) edition of *The Adventures of a Slave Girl* to him.[10]

Together, these works marked seminal shifts in Ottoman literature, introducing significant thematic and stylistic departures from earlier narrative traditions. Sezai's *Küçük Şeyler* (Little Things, 1891) – a pioneering collection of short stories that focused on the struggles of Istanbul's underdogs and marginalised figures, shaped the course of realist fiction in nineteenth-century Ottoman literature – and together with *Rumûzü'l-Edeb* (Secrets of Literature, 1898), a work reflecting his literary and cultural critiques, further extended his influence to a younger generation of writers, including Halit Ziya Uşaklıgil.

Sezai's early life, in some way, was shaped by a profound dilemma, despite coming from a privileged background and being born into a life of wealth and comfort. As an erudite and versatile young Ottoman intellectual, he was acutely aware of his mother's past as a slave from the Caucasus and of his household, which was staffed with dozens of domestic slaves. These included cooks, porters, stable men, nannies, *lala*s (manservants assigned to the care of a child), male servants and *cariye*s – female slaves in the Ottoman Empire – who attended to the intellectuals who gathered there to discuss these very ideas.[11]

Living in a household run by enslaved people, knowing that his own mother and many of his sisters-in-law had started their lives as slaves and witnessing the injustices inherent in the institution, Sezai grappled with the contradiction between the empire's westernisation efforts in addition to the reformist discussions carried out in his father's salon and this archaic form of human bondage.

Thanks to Güler Güven's meticulous research on Sezai and her interviews with his niece Samiye Bilhan, we know that accepting his mother's status as a former slave was especially difficult for Sezai. Whenever he voiced his frustrations, his mother Gülarayiş Hanım sought to console him, telling him that, had she not been enslaved, she would never have

[10] See Sezai's preface on page 1.

[11] Mümtaz, *Tarihimizde Hayal Olmuş Hakikatler*, p. 109. Mümtaz has given a detailed description of Sami Pasha's *konak* in Taşkasap, resembling a 'town' with more than sixty rooms where Sami Pasha lived with his two wives and thirteen children and their families. It seems that, in imagining and depicting the dilapidated old mansion in Chapter Four, where the female slave trader kept the Circassian *cariye*s, Sezai was inspired by his father's mansion.

had her children. From the same interview we learn that Sezai's distress over slavery was not limited to his mother's condition but stemmed from a genuine concern for all enslaved people. He often gathered the slaves in his family mansion and spoke to them about 'removing the cages, stepping out into the sunlight and to be free', tropes that would later appear repeatedly in *The Adventures of a Slave Girl*.[12] Sezai was also romantically involved with a *cariye* in his father's mansion. Güven, in her monograph on Sezai, describes this *cariye*, Vuslat, as 'Sezai's first love'.[13] Their romance, however, was cut short due to Sezai's short-lived marriage to Latife Hanım in 1885 during his first stay in Europe.[14] Vuslat died in 1888, the same year *The Adventures of a Slave Girl* was published. Three years later, in 1891, when Sezai published his famous short-story collection *Little Things*, there was a touching eulogy to Vuslat, titled 'Kitâbe-i Seng-i Mezar' (Epitaph), honouring her memory, in which he pleads with the universe to rescue Vuslat from under that tombstone and to tell 'his Vuslat that his life, unable to move beyond this stone, this frontier of dreams, has faded into oblivion'.[15]

Sezai's personal connection to slavery, shaped by his mother and Vuslat, places him in a unique position as a writer to address the subject. On one hand, he was the son of a Caucasian slave, growing up in a household where enslavement was an everyday reality; on the other, he was a Tanzimat intellectual steeped in the era's ideals of freedom and reform. His house itself reflected the era and the state of the empire: striving for modernisation while simultaneously bound to outdated systems, such as slavery, and failing or unwilling to recognize its role as an obstacle to progress.

Sezai lived in an era not only of political and cultural change and turmoil but also one of literary transformation. The Tanzimat era marked a turning point in Ottoman literary culture, as it witnessed the decline of

[12] Güven, *Sami Paşazade Sezayi ve Eserleri*. Güven's monograph on Samipaşazade Sezai, prepared under the guidance of Mehmet Kaplan, is not only an extensive and meticulously researched work but also the only study that provides a comprehensive account of the Samipaşazade family's history while offering detailed insights into Sezai's personal life and literary career.

[13] Ibid., p. 45.

[14] There is no information in Sezai's biographies about how he met Latife Hanım in Paris. However, we know that Latife Hanım's father, Tunuslu Mahmut Pasha, like Sezai's, owned a summer mansion in Çamlıca. The fact that this mansion is the subject of the story titled 'İki Yüz Elli Kuruşa bir Asır' (A Century for 250 Kuruş) in Sezai's *Küçük Şeyler* indicates that his acquaintance with Latife Hanım and her family dated back to Çamlıca. See Samipaşazade Sezai, *Bütün Eserleri*, pp. 114–18.

[15] Ibid., p. 132.

classical Ottoman literature and the emergence of European literary forms. Beginning in the second half of the nineteenth century, Ottoman readers were introduced to new literary genres such as the essay, the novel, the poem and the play from western literature, mainly through translations from French, followed by original Ottoman works in Armenian, Greek and Turkish.[16]

Among the literary forms introduced from Europe, the novel quickly became the most popular genre in the late-nineteenth-century Ottoman Empire.[17] In stark contrast to the ornate and formulaic storytelling of classical Ottoman literature, the novel provided Tanzimat writers, many of whom were western-educated bureaucrats and civil servants committed to progress, with new ways to explore contemporary issues. These early Ottoman writers all agreed on the didactic value of literature, often blurring the line between narrator and author to pass judgment on characters, convey information and reinforce moral or political lessons. Despite their shared commitment to literature as a tool for education, however, their objectives varied. Take, for instance, two of the earliest and most influential novelists: Namık Kemal (1840–88) – writer, intellectual, reformer, journalist, playwright and political activist – and Ahmet Mithat (1844–1912) – educator, publisher, translator and the most prolific Ottoman novelist. Namık Kemal, an advocate for constitutionalism and political freedom, sought to instil patriotic and reformist ideals, while Ahmet Mithat avoided direct political engagement, instead using his prolific output to broaden the general knowledge of his readers.

[16] Among them were: Hovsep Vartanyan (1816–79), an Ottoman Armenian statesman, writer and journalist, also known as Vartan Pasha, who wrote the first original Ottoman novel, *Akabi Hikayesi* (The Story of Akabi), in Armeno-Turkish in 1851; Şemseddin Sami Frashëri (1850–1904), an Ottoman Albanian intellectual, linguist and philosopher, whose *Taaşşuk-i Talât ve Fitnat* (The Romance of Talât and Fitnat, 1872) became one of the earliest examples of the Ottoman novel; the Ottoman Greek writer, journalist and translator Evangelinos Misailidis (1820–90) who published his Ottoman-Turkish novel (in Greek script) *Temaşa-i Dünya ve Cefakar u Cefakeş* in 1870; and Namık Kemal (1840–88), one of the most influential figures of the nineteenth century – a writer, intellectual, reformer, journalist, playwright and political activist – followed with *İntibah yahut Sergüzeşt-i Ali Bey* (Awakening, or the Adventure of Ali Bey, 1874). For more on the multi-lingual nature of the Tanzimat era, see Uslu and Altuğ (eds), *Tanzimat ve Edebiyat*.

[17] The number of novels, both translated and original, published in the Ottoman Empire between 1859 and 1900 exceeds 1,000. For a detailed discussion on the topic and an extensive catalogue of novels published between 1840 and 1940, see Ahu Selin Erkul Yağcı, *Turkey's Reading (R)evolution: A Study on Books, Readers and Translation, 1840–1940* (unpubl. PhD diss., Boğaziçi University, 2011), p. 76.

The early novels, published between 1870 and 1890, drawing equally on European literary models and traditional Ottoman narratives, consistently explored excessively sentimental tragic themes: fatal illnesses, ill-fated arranged marriages, the social and romantic constraints of gender segregation and love stories destined for heartbreak. Unrequited love, romances built on improbable, almost Shakespearean coincidences and arranged marriages were especially common. Another recurring theme was the ongoing tension between tradition and westernisation and at times between the true Ottoman man and his superfluous, overly westernised version – the *alafranga* dandy – representing the anxieties and criticisms of excessive western influence.[18] Alongside these broader cultural concerns, slavery emerged as a distinctively Ottoman and deeply local theme in early novels.

Despite ongoing global abolitionist movements and the growing prominence of *hürriyet* (freedom) in Ottoman intellectual discourse, shaped by engagement with European political thought and the ideals of French Revolution,[19] Tanzimat writers, rather than adopting an abolitionist stance akin to Harriet Beecher Stowe's (1811–96) anti-slavery novel *Uncle Tom's Cabin* (1852), chose to depict slavery primarily as yet another tragic theme.

[18] A different version of this character first emerged in Namık Kemal's *İntibah* (Awakening, 1876) as the spendthrift orphan, whose lack of parental guidance and reckless spending lead to the downfall of his household. Later, the character evolved into the infamous *alafranga* dandy, a figure both ridiculed and critiqued for his excessive imitation of European lifestyles, particularly in Ahmet Mithat's *Felâtun Bey and Rakım Efendi* (1875), Hüseyin Rahmi Gürpınar's *Şık* (Chic, 1889) and Recaizade Mahmut Ekrem's *Araba Sevdası* (The Carriage Affair, 1896). For more on the *alafranga* dandy, see Parla, *Babalar ve Oğullar*; Gürbilek, 'Dandies and Originals', p. 612.

[19] Prominent figures of the Tanzimat and the Young Ottomans, such as Ziya Pasha (1829–80) – a writer, administrator, leading member of the Young Ottomans and translator (as well as devoted admirer) of Jean-Jacques Rousseau, who in the second issue of the newspaper *Hürriyet*, an opposition newspaper serving as the voice of the Young Ottomans published in London between 1868 and 1870, wrote that '*Hürriyet* is the most beautiful divine blessing' (Topal and Karlıtekin, *Sürgünde Muhalefet*, p. 8) – and Namık Kemal (1840–88) – one of the most influential figures of the nineteenth century, a writer, intellectual, reformer, journalist, playwright and political activist, who wrote in his article titled 'Medeniyet' (Civilization) that 'a person's right and purpose are not merely to live, but to live in freedom' (Kaplan et al., *Yeni Türk Edebiyatı Antolojisi, 1865–1876*, vol. II, p. 233) – played crucial roles in expanding the notion of *hürriyet* beyond its traditional legal connotations, emphasising its necessity for national progress and self-governance. However, the Tanzimat notion of *hürriyet* remained limited mostly to political freedoms, rather than extending to broader concepts of personal autonomy or the *de facto* abolition of slavery.

As İsmail Parlatır has highlighted in his pioneering work *Tanzimat Edebiyatında Kölelik* (Slavery in Tanzimat Literature), slavery-related news frequently appeared in Ottoman newspapers of the time, covering issues such as the status of enslaved people within the empire, the fate of Circassian slaves and global abolitionist efforts, particularly in the United States and the British Empire.[20] Tanzimat writers, given their deep involvement in journalism, were undoubtedly aware of these discussions and occasionally even contributed opinion pieces on the topic. However, even as global debates on abolition had gained momentum and there was pressure on the Ottoman government to curtail the slave trade throughout the 1880s and 1890s, for the Tanzimat novelists slavery remained a peripheral motif, a mere literary device for romantic or melodramatic plots.

While *hürriyet* (freedom) was championed as a fundamental right and frequently explored in newly adopted literary forms such as poetry and plays, its extension to enslaved individuals in novels was scarce. Enslaved women, particularly *cariye*s, often appeared only as minor characters, serving, in Deniz Kandiyoti's words, as 'tame sexual slaves', Ottoman male writers' 'conventional response to young men's appetites'.[21] This omission is particularly striking given that some Tanzimat-era writers were not only aware of discussions surrounding slavery but had direct personal connections to it: some writers' mothers had been brought to Istanbul as slaves, and some, such as the pioneering woman writer Fatma Aliye, were slave owners.[22]

To further elaborate, for prominent Tanzimat writers such as Ahmet Mithat and Abdülhak Hamit Tarhan (1852–1937), whose mothers, like Sezai's, were once Circassian slaves, slavery never emerged as a subject of serious critique. In his 1913 poem 'Validem' (My Mother), written upon his mother's death, Tarhan portrayed her life – including her enslavement – in a highly sentimental manner. Ahmet Mithat held a conflicted stance on slavery. On the one hand, he believed that depriving a person of their freedom was contrary to civilisation and morality; on the other, he frequently depicted Ottoman slavery as humane, particularly in contrast to western slavery, and he even presented it as advantageous for enslaved Circassian women, framing it as a match-making mechanism or a path to social mobility. In his seminal novel *Felâtun Bey and Rakım Efendi*, he goes so far as to have Margaret, a British woman receiving

[20] Parlatır, *Tanzimat Edebiyatında Kölelik*, pp. 23–30.

[21] Kandiyoti, 'Slave Girls, Temptresses, and Comrades', p. 39.

[22] See Appendix E for the archival document depicting Fatma Aliye's purchase of a Circassian slave woman.

Turkish lessons from Rakım Efendi, express fascination with Ottoman servitude upon meeting Canan, Rakım Efendi's slave, exclaiming: 'My, this is just like a dream! I'd want to be a slave like this'.[23]

Similar sentiments echoed also in the writings of Fatma Aliye (1862–1936), one of the few early Ottoman woman writers, the daughter of prominent historian and statesman Ahmet Cevdet Pasha and a protégé of Ahmet Mithat. In her *Women of Islam*, (1891), a corrective to western misconceptions about Muslim women, she does not explicitly advocate for slavery yet presents it as benevolent toward women. Curiously, her fictitious European woman character Madame F, almost mirroring Ahmet Mithat's Margaret, justly remarks: 'But Madame, you have described slavery in such glowing terms that all will aspire to be a slave'.[24]

This begs the question of where *The Adventures of a Slave Girl* stands within the landscape of Tanzimat-era novels. Published in 1888, Samipaşazade Sezai's *The Adventures of a Slave Girl* is undoubtedly one of the most significant novels of the later Tanzimat period, for its stylistic and narrative qualities. It sits at a crossroads, drawing on the themes and stylistic choices of earlier works. But it also signals a shift in how Tanzimat ideas of freedom could be extended to subjects marginalised by society, such as female slaves.

The Adventures of a Slave Girl *as a Tanzimat novel*

Set against the rapidly changing socio-political landscape of late-nineteenth-century Istanbul, *The Adventures of a Slave Girl* follows the poignant journey of Dilber, a young Circassian girl abducted from her homeland and sold into slavery in the Ottoman Empire. At first, one could just as easily call it a stereotypical Tanzimat novel, a tragic love story between a Circassian slave girl *cariye* and the highly westernised, Paris-educated young *bey* of the household, whose romance is sabotaged by his family, inevitably paving the way for tragedy. As such, the novel encompasses all the quintessential themes of Tanzimat literature: tragic romance, slavery, the westernised young Ottoman man and the unfortunate consequences of arranged marriages. However, while Sezai employed these familiar tropes, he repurposed them to craft a novel that feels both recognizable and strikingly different as it exhausts and

[23] Ahmet Mithat, *Felâtun Bey and Râkım Efendi*, p. 108. Ahmet Mithat furthered his comparison of western and Ottoman (or eastern) slavery in his novel *Acaib-i Alem*.

[24] Fatma Aliye, *Women of Islam*, p. 18.

subverts existing literary tropes. This can be best seen in Sezai's portrayal of the protagonist, Dilber. Despite the suffocating constraints of her bondage and the vulnerability of her youth, Dilber repeatedly refuses to surrender to fate. She fights against the chains of slavery, daring to dream of freedom, plotting her escape even as a small child and later defiantly pushing back against the orientalist gaze that seeks to define her. Perhaps, one could argue, in doing so, Sezai not only allows Dilber to resist her captors but also challenges his readers, forcing them to confront the illusions that had long framed Ottoman slavery as charitable or as a pathway to social mobility, a misleading justification perpetuated and defended by his contemporaries.

Moreover, Sezai reimagined the westernised Ottoman man, moving beyond the familiar tropes that had long dominated Tanzimat literature. Celal Bey is neither the reckless spendthrift, like Namık Kemal's Ali Bey in *İntibah* (Awakening), whose lack of discipline and proper guidance leads to his family's ruin, nor is he a shallow caricature of excessive westernisation, like Ahmet Mithat's Felâtun Bey in *Felâtun Bey and Rakım Efendi* or Recaizade Mahmut Ekrem's Bihruz Bey in *Araba Sevdası* (The Carriage Affair), with their ostentatious fashion, pretentious command of French and uprooted identities. Instead, Celal Bey's westernisation is something more unsettling: a westernised Ottoman man whose transformation is not merely external but deeply internalised. A Paris-educated painter and apprentice to the renowned nineteenth-century French orientalist Jean-Léon Gérôme (1824–1904), Celal does not simply adopt European manners; he adopts a European gaze. He does not just adapt western sophistication; he internalises its perspective, looking upon his own people through an orientalist lens. His westernisation is not performed; it is engrained, and it is through this lens that he perceives and, ultimately, fails Dilber.

Nowhere is this more evident than in Celal's portrayal of Dilber, whom he insists on painting through the lens of European exoticisation. His gaze, his perception of the world around him and, in this case, Dilber, operates on two levels: first as an artist and second as a Tanzimat man. Through this portrayal, Sezai offers a twofold critique. First, he exposes the Tanzimat elite's wilful blindness to slavery. Celal lives in a mansion in the Moda district, where the salon is adorned with paintings of both Napoleon (1769–1821) and Sultan Mehmet the Conqueror (r. 1444–46, 1451–81) and Anatolian rugs – eastern and western art, attesting to a trendy amalgamation of eastern and European aesthetics of the times. He is surrounded by French governesses, piano teachers and enslaved servants, yet despite being an heir to this world and embodying the ideals of the western-educated Ottoman elite, he fails to recognize the conflict around him.

Sezai's depictions, not only of this salon but also of the family members within it, serve as striking reflections of the era's inherent duality. In the novel, this Tanzimat-era salon unfolds like a tableau reminiscent of a British drawing room: Zehra Hanım and Asaf Bey play cards as they listen to their daughter at the piano, while Celal reads books or leafs through European magazines with the French governess. Yet, despite Zehra Hanım and Asaf Bey embracing certain aspects of modernity, engaging together in leisurely card games or employing a French governess, their deeply rooted traditional views on marriage and slavery, as we later learn, stand in stark contrast to their public-facing performance of modernity. This contrast is also present in the case of Celal's younger sister, a well-educated and talented modern piano-player whose marriage to someone of her parents' choice has been arranged for wealth and social advancement, further exposing the duplicity embedded within this ostensibly progressive household.

Throughout the novel, Sezai subtly signals that this duplicity is not confined to the family mansion but extends to the broader Ottoman intellectual and cultural milieu. The female slave trader praises Dilber's skill on the lute (oud) before selling her to Asaf Bey's household, yet it soon becomes apparent that this classical Ottoman instrument holds no significance in the Ottoman household; only the piano prevails as the chosen symbol of modernisation. Later in the story, we will see that only on the periphery of the empire, in Egypt, the *cariye*s and the odalisques play the oud. Sezai makes his scepticism of modernity and reform explicit through his depiction of Celal's uncle Münevver Bey's salon, where Celal's cousin performs a piece from the then-popular *Faust* opera to a seemingly interested audience with a refined taste in western classical music, only for the same space, minutes later, to host a heated debate on the uncle's mistrust and critique of modern – namely, European – science and thought. Therefore, Celal's inability to acknowledge Dilber as an enslaved subject reflects not just his personal blindness but the broader paradox of the Tanzimat era, an empire that prided itself on modernisation while continuing to uphold archaic institutions such as slavery.

At the same time, Sezai extends his critique beyond the Ottoman elite to European orientalists, who, like Celal, refuse to see slavery for what it truly is. At first, Celal's Europeanised gaze does not recognize Dilber as an enslaved girl suffering under an oppressive system; instead, he sees her as an aestheticised object, a romanticised Circassian beauty, a mere prop for his next painting. This idealised vision, rooted in fantasies of submission and desirability, mirrors western orientalists' fascination with the fair Circassian and the harem and reinforces the distorted narratives shared by both Ottoman and European observers. Sezai dismantles this notion by allowing Dilber to resist, to challenge Celal's expectations and rupture these orientalist portrayals. In doing so, he critiques not only the hypocrisy of the Tanzimat elite but also the complicity of European perspectives that exoticise and depoliticise the realities of enslavement. Sezai gives agency to a previously passive and helpless character, Dilber, enabling her to shift another character's perspective on slavery – namely, Celal Bey's. In this, the novel secures for itself a distinct place within Tanzimat-era novels, but this does not mean it is unilaterally anti-slavery.

Celal's repeated attempts to transform Dilber into the idealised 'fair Circassian' on his canvas parallel the ways in which both Ottoman and orientalist perspectives romanticised slavery rather than reckoning with its realities. Yet Dilber, in an unprecedented way, refuses to perform the role assigned to her, both in Celal's paintings and in his mind, forcing him and the reader to confront the limits of their own perception.

Dilber's refusal to submit ultimately fractures Celal's gaze. In this moment, Sezai once again diverges from the conventions of Tanzimat novels, allowing his character not just to experience love or loss but to grow, to evolve from his initial perspective of Dilber and slavery, and to reveal to us his emotional arc – an unprecedented move in a Tanzimat novel since the majority of them feature characters without depth, whose inner worlds are inaccessible to the reader. In the same vein, Celal does not fall in love with Dilber at first sight, as customary in many novels of the period, nor is she merely a passive beauty or fleeting distraction. Instead, his affection develops as he begins to truly see her, not merely as an aestheticised figure, but as a strong young woman who, despite a life shaped by tragedy, has never relinquished her sense of agency and dignity.

In making Celal and Dilber's love story a realistic albeit tragic one, Sezai reimagines the romantic tropes of Tanzimat literature, demonstrating that *cariye*s are more than minor characters drawn into the plots only to enable romantic interactions in novels set within a segregated society. Likewise, arranged marriages in Tanzimat literature are often depicted as conduits of misfortune, but Sezai repositions yet another way to explore the evolving notions of freedom and its limitations within the ideological framework of the Tanzimat era. By granting one character the agency to resist and the other the capacity to grow, Sezai envisions an alternative Tanzimat novel, one that may not be explicitly abolitionist, but one that is undeniably anti-slavery.

The Adventures of a Slave Girl *as an Anti-slavery Novel*

> Poor children! Your tiny little hands were not meant to break the chains of slavery – a burden of ancient Asian civilisations – that crushed humanity under its oppressive weight for centuries. Your hands were meant to stroke the feathers of little birds and caress the petals of flowers, as delicate as yourselves.
>
> Sezai, *The Adventures of a Slave Girl*, p. 51.

Let us dwell on the question of why *The Adventures of a Slave Girl* is an anti-slavery novel. The most direct answer to that question is in Sezai's preface to the 1924 edition of the novel.[25] In his preface, Sezai – perhaps writing from the vantage point of the newly established Turkish Republic, or perhaps nostalgically harkening back to the late-nineteenth-century Ottoman literary world – discusses the enthusiastic reception of the novel by the young reformists and the contrasting suspicion and scrutiny that it instigated in the imperial palace. Thus, he noted:

> In 1888, the Ottoman Empire had been in a thirty-three-year-long night with no hope of dawn, not a glimmer of light on the horizon. The few stars that appeared in the sky during this prolonged darkness had left their homeland, vanishing into the horizons of distant, foreign lands. Those that remained briefly flickered in the homeland sky before being engulfed by the black fog rising from the volcanoes of *istibdad*. During that period, the natural course of intellectual life was disrupted by ideological conflict and inner turmoil, spreading from individuals to society, from society to nations, and from nations to the entire homeland. There was no peaceful corner left in the entire homeland where one could immerse oneself in literature. These events affected me as well. I was suffocated by the crushing, raging, ruinous restlessness of the times. Whenever I sat at my desk for the muse to honour and grace my poems, I would hear the footsteps of spies at my door, their predatory, tiger-like eyes watching through my window. For I had started *The Adventures of a Slave Girl* in opposition to slavery and concluded it with 'to her freedom' (pp. 29–30).

Sezai's close analysis of the political and social circumstances epitomises previously discussed traits of early Tanzimat writers – that is, the mission of freedom and liberty – not only as abstract western concepts, imported media of reforms and reorganisation in the empire, but as discourses that stand on acute social and cultural observations, detecting discrepancies, hypocrisies and deeply rooted inequalities in the domestic spheres across socio-economic classes. It is in this context that Sezai's introduction provides insight into why the novel is an anti-slavery Ottoman novel rather

[25] See pp. 29–30 for Sezai's preface.

than just a tragic or melodramatic romance between a slave girl and the son of the slave master. The narrator is consistent in the novel and dictates that standing up against slavery needs to be every individual's ethical stance in the empire. Slave dealers, owners and even enslaved characters such as Taravet who participate in sustaining the system are all subject to the narrator's harsh scrutiny and critique. Indeed, freedom is not merely a matter of legal reform for Sezai but also a moral issue. In this sense, unravelling the deeply rooted, ubiquitous and pervasive practice of female slavery among all socio-economic classes lies at the heart of Sezai's novel.

However, Samipaşazade Sezai's anti-slavery stance appears to falter, especially for the modern reader, in his depiction of Taravet, the Black enslaved girl in the first household to which Dilber is sold. Taravet is rendered through a vocabulary of hostility that repeatedly foregrounds her skin colour and associates her with cruelty and malice, at times bordering on caricature. Such portrayals of Black enslaved figures as morally distorted or excessively harsh are not uncommon in Tanzimat literature. One of the most extreme examples appears in a work by Sezai's mentor, Namık Kemal, whose posthumously published play *Kara Bela* (Black Trouble, 1908) demonises an African eunuch so thoroughly that the work was criticised not only for its weak literary merit but also for its overt hostility towards eunuchs. In response, Şahabettin Süleyman, a prominent figure of the *Fecr-i Ati* (Dawn of the Future) group, wrote *Siyah Süs* (Black Ornament), a non-extant play widely known to have been written as direct counter to Namık Kemal's representation. In *Felâtun Bey and Rakım Efendi*, Ahmet Mithat presented Fedai as a nurturing surrogate mother who raises Rakım into an exemplary young Ottoman man, effectively entrusting the moral future of the empire to an African enslaved woman. Yet the same author also created one of the most malevolent figures in Ottoman fiction, the eunuch Mesut, in *Dünyaya İkinci Geliş yahut İstanbul'da Neler Olmuş?* (A Return to the World, or What Happened in Istanbul?). In this diverse literary representation of Black slaves, Sezai's portrayal of Taravet may initially appear to reproduce a familiar pattern of racial demonisation. Yet Taravet is not the novel's only Black character. Cevher, the African eunuch in the Egyptian merchant's household, is depicted in markedly different terms: empathetic, morally perceptive and ultimately self-sacrificing in his efforts to secure Dilber's freedom. A closer reading thus suggests that the narrative's hostility toward Taravet is less a function of her race alone than of her active complicity in the mechanisms of domestic enslavement. Unlike the other enslaved girls whom Dilber encounters in the novel, Taravet aligns herself with her master, participating in the inspection of Dilber's body to reduce her price and subjecting her to physical exhaustion and verbal abuse, at times exceeding the master's own cruelty. Cevher, by contrast, expresses discomfort with enslavement, recognizes Dilber's suffering and ultimately dares to defy his master on her behalf. Seen in this light, Sezai's treatment of Taravet may be read as both racial condemnation of her Blackness and morally charged differentiation between characters based on their relationship to the institution of slavery itself, a distinction that complicates the narrative's racial politics without fully resolving them.

Marriage and Enslavement in the Novel

Dilber may be the protagonist in the novel, but she is one of the many enslaved girls and boys in the empire. Taravet, often referred to as 'the Arab slave' in the novel, is persistently described with racial attributes, with an emphasis on her dark skin, revealing the inherent racism against black slaves. Dilber and Çaresaz are both Circassian female slaves who work as domestic help, like Taravet. The nameless so-called 'Circassian gems' in the opening scene of the novel are *cariye*s who are sold off to the harem of wealthier Ottomans. And, finally, Cevher is a Sudanese eunuch, kidnapped, castrated and sold to a wealthy Egyptian household. In addition to individual characters, there are also references to enslaved groups of Circassian girls who are in the hands of slave traders and sold off as odalisques – in other words, concubines – to private harems or as domestic workers to middle-class households.

In unveiling the anatomy of female slavery in the empire, Sezai first and foremost unravels the systemic oppression of female slaves, and more significantly the hypocrisy of the pro-reformists in the empire. Early in the novel, in Chapter Two, Sezai interjects as the anti-slavery, compassionate narrator:

> Poor children! Your tiny little hands were not meant to break the chains of slavery – a burden of ancient Asian civilisations – that crushed humanity under its oppressive weight for centuries. Your hands were meant to stroke the feathers of little birds and caress the petals of flowers, as delicate as yourselves (p. 51).

In this quotation, slavery is presented as an oriental plague, persistent and detrimental to humanity, still haunting the children in a world that has turned its helm westward. While Sezai traces it back to ancient Asian civilisations, implying its old eastern roots, he bitterly acknowledges that slavery continues to rear its ugly head in the Ottoman Empire. A similar philosophical interjection occurs in Chapter Seven, where Sezai addresses slavery within the context of marriage but moving beyond the conventional Tanzimat-era trope of determining who may marry whom. For him, this is not merely a simplistic question of whether a slave girl can marry a free man, a more common motif in Tanzimat novels such as Ahmet Mithat's *Dünyaya İkinci Geliş yahut İstanbul'da Neler Olmuş?* (A Return to the World, or What Happened in Istanbul?) of 1875, but rather a deeper critique of structural inequalities in society. In Chapter Eleven, Sezai stages a conversation between the young, educated and modern Celal Bey and his conservative uncle, Münevver Bey, centring on the freedom to love. Münevver Bey, raised as a devout Muslim, is sceptical of modern science and resistant to the promises of modernity. His dogmatic ideas lead to a fundamental clash with Celal over the topic of love, free will and marriage. The uncle staunchly defends arranged marriages – unions overseen by parents – and dismisses young people's romantic aspirations as irrational and driven by inexperience. Sezai makes the uncle uphold and explicitly articulate the conventional maxim of the time: 'Everyone should marry their equal' (p. 98).

In this context, the uncle's use of the Arabic word 'küfv' (كفو), which in English translation means 'equal', is a deliberate choice, as it underscores the uncle's essentialist belief in the inherent inequality between a slave girl and a free person. Celal, in contrast, champions individual freedom and challenges the injustice embedded in his uncle's rigid notion of equality; he retorts: 'I would say that the most important freedom that young people have in this world is to marry whomever they desire. After all, is it not the greatest injustice in the world to interfere with one's freedom to choose a partner, the heart's liberty to decide and the soul's natural inclination to be attracted?' (p. 98). Celal Bey's concept of a person's right is antithetical to Münevver Bey's idea of equality, and their conversation reveals more than a generational conflict over tradition and modernity. The debate over marriage exposes the contradictions within Tanzimat-era notions of freedom, revealing its racial, sexual and ethnic biases, and ultimately highlights the incompatibility of slavery and freedom.

Language and Enslavement

In addition to marriage, the novel's portrayal of language sheds light on the master-slave discourse. In the novel, Circassian slave girls are strictly forbidden from gathering and conversing in their native language – an offense punishable by whipping at the hands of the slave master. Yet, the novel reveals the persistent presence of the mother tongue, appearing in dreams and in private conversations, alongside the forced acquisition of

Turkish, the oppressor's language. Circassian in the novel thus emerges as the language of empowerment for the enslaved girls, and Turkish becomes the language of the oppressor. For instance, in the first household, Dilber is given the very Turkish name 'Dilber' by the mistress and starts to learn Turkish. The narrator ascribes this to a universal linguistic aptitude first: 'As weeks and months passed, Dilber started to speak and understand Turkish with the remarkable skill that most children have in learning new languages' (p. 46), but thereafter the narrator juxtaposes the language acquisition with enslavement and force. Despite her ability to pick up Turkish as a child, this is not a choice for Dilber. In the slave trader's house, we get a closer look at this oppressive control of language: 'In Hajji Ömer's house, the slave girls would gather in one room in the evenings and talk to each other. However, laughing too much and speaking in Circassian were forbidden, and if a girl was returned by a customer, for whatever reason, she would receive ten to fifteen lashes' (p. 40). In other words, oppression is manifested not only in the prohibition of the use of the mother tongue, but also in the forced substitution of Turkish as the language of submission and hegemony.

Realism, Homeland and Memory

The transactional and therefore inhumane nature of slavery is most attentively portrayed and criticised by Sezai. In this sense, it is not a coincidence that the novel starts with the arrival of the slave ship sailing from Batum to the Tophane Harbour in Istanbul. The novel thus starts with the declaration of the established Black Sea slave routes and unravels the slave trading network that sustains it. In the dry and realistic transaction scene on the first page, girls are sold off as commodities, and the slave trader is described as a ghoul, a scary monster, whose whip is the primary tool of his business, and who feeds off the misery of young girls. Sezai carefully creates an ethos based on slave traders, slave houses, maritime networks and established slave routes, all of which sustain the cycle of slavery. In this dark world, Dilber is seen as a source of profit, fed and taken care of solely to raise her market value, which is carefully calculated by the slave traders in the novel. Her price is negotiated; her value is reassessed with intrusive health checks. In Chapter One, in the first house to which she is sold, the narrator describes the examination and negotiation scene:

> First, the mistress patted down every inch of her body and found many defects. Of course, these were just petty excuses to lower her price. Then, the Arab

> slave girl conducted her own thorough examination and said: 'Ma'am, she is useless. Too skinny. She won't survive'. Their greedy and selfish bargaining over how to exploit a human being lasted for hours, before they finally settled on forty liras as the sale price for the slave girl (p. 44).

Sezai's realistic depiction of Dilber's sale in this scene is followed by a depiction of the indenture signed by the slave trader and the buyer. The deliberate textual details on the operation of the slave trade in the empire reveal the dehumanisation of Dilber, but more significantly the inhumanity of slavery itself. After negotiations are completed, the parties sign the following agreement on the sale of Dilber:

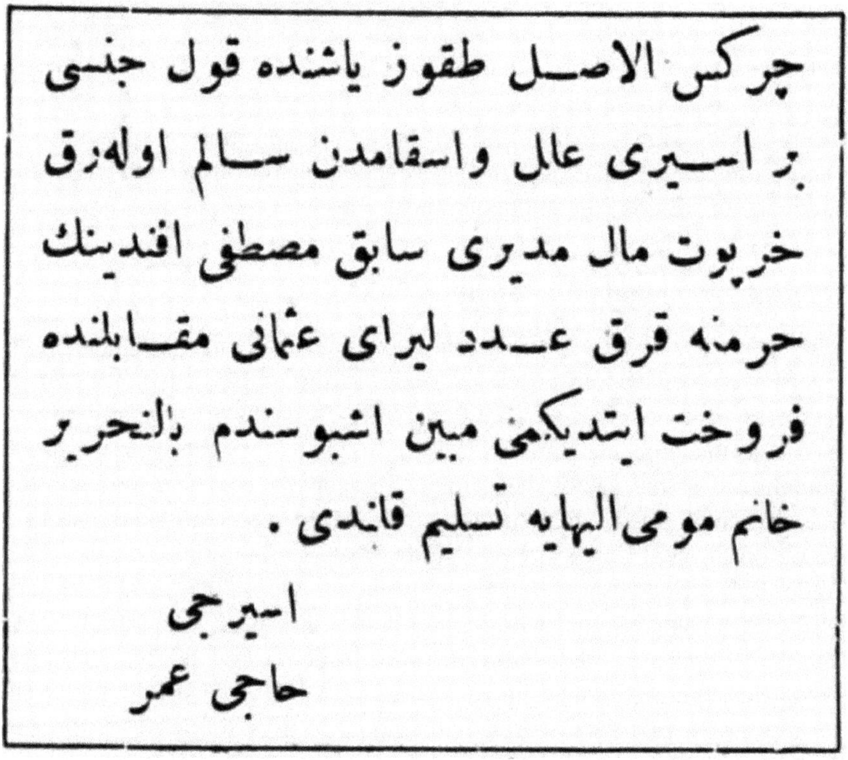
چرکس الاصل طقوز یاشنده قول جنسی
بر اسیری علل واسقامدن سالم اوله‌رق
خربوت مال مدیری سابق مصطفی افندینک
حرمنه قرق عدد لیرای عثمانی مقابلنده
فروخت ایتدیکمی مبین اشبو سندم بالتحریر
خانم مومی الیهایه تسلیم قلندی .
اسیرجی
حاجی عمر

Figure 1 Dilber's slave contract.'This contract hereby is to declare that I have sold a slave of Circassian origin, aged nine, free of any illness or defect, for the sum of forty Ottoman liras to the wife of Mustafa Efendi, former Fiscal Director of Harput. The deed is written and handed over to the afore-mentioned lady to certify the transaction. Slave Trader Hajji Ömer'.

It is important to note that such indentures were prevalent throughout the Ottoman Empire during this period. Despite international agreements and domestic reforms, slavery remained a common practice, and stories like Dilber's were far from anomalies. The archival sources in Appendices A–E attest to the ubiquitous sale of female Circassian teenage slaves by slave traders during this time.

Defying the Fair Circassian Trope

But Sezai does not stop at the first sale of Dilber. He continues to narrate how her price increases every time she is sold off to a new master. As the indenture above shows, she is first sold for forty liras, then for sixty-five and, eventually, for 150 liras to Asaf Pasha's mansion, before getting sold off to a merchant in Egypt. At the end of Chapter Three, when Dilber is sold for sixty-five liras, the narrator compassionately yet sarcastically comments on how her masters profited from her sale:

> Poor Dilber! Just as she had endured all kinds of torment when Mustafa Efendi was out of work – carrying the weight of the entire house on her tiny shoulders – she was once again put to work, this time to pay for Mustafa Efendi's debts and travel expenses with her frail body (pp. 56–7).

Even the elderly woman in whose house Dilber seeks refuge in Chapter Two understands that she cannot truly free her without purchasing her from her current master. In a heartbreaking scene, Sezai depicts how the old woman approaches the brutal mistress and Mustafa Efendi to make an offer:

> The old woman continued talking. 'My girl, just as God forgives the sins of children, mistresses should excuse their mistakes. I came here to plead with you. Allow me to give you the five pouches of silver coins that I have saved, and you give me the girl in return', she suggested.
>
> 'What are you going to do with her?' the mistress asked. The old woman attempted a light-hearted reply, trying to resolve the situation in her favour. 'I will free a bird on Holy Night', she said with a twinkle in her eyes. 'I am not selling my slave to anyone', said the mistress in her usual unpleasant way (p. 53).

The novel's audacity to realistically unveil the brutality of slavery is also present in the depiction of Istanbul as a city complicit in this system. In this city, the pastoral hills and the mesmerising, bucolic Bosphorus shores exist alongside dark and perilous corners. The Istanbul we recognize from the Ottoman romantic novels, with its idyllic hills, landscapes and picturesque promenades, are absent in the opening pages of the novel. Instead, the Istanbul where Dilber is brought is hostile, especially for those forced to live in it as enslaved people. It is neither a home nor a homeland; it is a prison. In fact, they are forced to live in the slave traders' dilapidated houses, likened to scary dungeons.

Another singular trait about the novel, one that is contrasted with the dark and brutal depiction of Istanbul, is the persistent remembrance of the Caucasus. Neither life in Istanbul nor Egypt can obliterate the sweet memory of the homeland in the minds of the enslaved girls. In this sense, Sezai creates a space for the memory of a homeland for the slave girls. This longing is particularly evident in the beginning of Chapter Six, when Celal Bey asks Dilber about her origins: 'Where are you from, İzmit or the Caucasus? Take a look at the dark green trees, the forests over there; look at the blue skies with your black eyes. Did you come from a land of such colours?' (p. 67) His knowledge of the Caucasus is second-hand, likely gleaned from paintings – he is, after all, a Paris-educated painter. He asks Dilber to look around, finding a similarity between Istanbul and the Caucasus inspired by his own colour palette. But for Dilber, the connection is neither seamless nor convincing. The Caucasus and Istanbul exist in an uneasy relationship, beyond the colour associations, the romanticised, exotic aesthetics that Celal, with his Europeanised vision, can offer. To him, the Caucasus is an image, one that he might have seen in popular travelogues; to her, it is an irretrievable past.

In one of the key passages in the novel, Circassian slave girls violate one of the most important house rules of the slave trader and secretly gather to reminisce about their homeland in their native Circassian. Sezai describes the scene in great detail:

> They conversed enthusiastically about the Caucasus, remembering its towering mountains whose peaks almost grazed the blue skies, its enchanting wild forests where morning birds were singing all kinds of songs; its colourful rivers mirroring nearby flowers, meadows and clouds, as they flowed gracefully from the peaks. They reminisced about its crystal-clear waters cascading in a rhythm, nourishing the soul, and the joy and delights of dancing to the tunes that they played on their traditional instruments along the riverbanks (p. 61).

In this passage, the slave girls are portrayed as doing two critical things: going against the brutal rules of the slave trader and congregating to talk in their native language; remembering and therefore reifying the distant memory of a faraway home, establishing a shared history. On both accounts, the presence of a homeland is empowering for the slave girls. In the same scene, one of the slave girls says:

> Those happy days, the cheerful dreams, the sweet memories… As I watch them pass before my eyes these past few days, my restless heart longs to follow in their wake. Oh, how I miss everything, even the trees in my childhood home.

> Only now do I realise that the rose bush in our garden was more than a rose bush; it was my friend. All the rooms, every single corner in that house, all the faces around me were a part of my childhood, part of a happy time in my life. And now, look at me. I am being sold to a stranger, to an unfamiliar household (p. 62).

The presence of homesickness, the persistent memory of a distant homeland and the Circassian slave girls' refusal to accept Istanbul as a home deconstruct the existing Tanzimat literary narratives about life as a slave in Istanbul being better and, hence, preferable to a miserable life in the homeland. At times, Sezai narrates homesickness as a nostalgic sentiment. When the brutal slave trader Hajji Ömer and Dilber cross the Galata Bridge in the beginning of the novel, Dilber pauses for a moment on the bridge. This is the first time she catches a sight of the new city. As an eight-year-old, severed from her homeland and mother, starving and ill-treated, she is overcome by a sense of homesickness. Sezai narrates the moment in romantic albeit critical terms:

> On the Galata Bridge, her eyes were fixed on the steamboats, docking and departing on either side of the bridge. After a few more steps, the instant the sound of a steamer's whistle reached her, a shiver seized her entire body, for the echo of a steamer's whistle in Batum, which had taken her from her homeland, still lingered in her memory. A breeze blowing from the mountains that stood shoulder to shoulder on the horizon, beneath a blue sky, swept across her hair, reminding her of a dream she once had – a dream of her homeland – and offering her aching heart a strange solace (p. 41).

Istanbul in this novel is no longer the Istanbul of fancy oxcart rides, public outings, French dialogues, Parisian hairdos and trivial romances. Instead, it is a gloomy city, at times narrated with a gothic tone, with owls, spectres, a haunting past and present, as a world of sadness and nostalgia, as a city of not belonging, a city of captivity. We see a similar attempt in the realistic depiction of Dilber. Sezai shows no will or desire to depict her as a Circassian beauty, nor to beautify her. In fact, early in the novel, she is emphatically described as being ugly by the slave traders, one of them saying outright to the buyer that she would sell Dilber for more if she had been more beautiful. Celal, who insists on painting Dilber as a stereotypical exotic, fair Circassian beauty in his paintings soon realises that the Dilber in front of him is a human being who feels, suffers and longs to break her chains. The subject of beauty in this case is significant for two reasons: the first is that it is antithetical to the prominent Circassian fair beauty trope. Dilber rebels against and resists this stereotype vehemently when sold off to the harem of a wealthy man in Egypt where she is forced to perform the role of the oriental and exotic Circassian fair beauty. But even in that moment of imprisonment and captivity, Dilber escapes Egypt and throws herself into the wild waters of the River Nile rather than perform the predestined role of an odalisque. But Sezai gives us foreboding clues of Dilber's rebellion against this imposed identity much earlier in the novel. Celal Bey, the painter and Asaf Pasha's only son, uses Dilber as a model for his paintings. The paintings, intricately described in the novel, are made after the tradition of the nineteenth-century orientalist paintings of Circassian fair beauties. But as the following excerpt reveals, Dilber deeply resents being portrayed as 'that girl' in the paintings and refuses to perform the role of that oriental stereotype. She feels humiliated by the orientalist painter's gaze and by being objectified. Sezai unravels Celal's superficial and two-dimensional creation of Dilber:

> Never one to leave her alone, Celal Bey quickly made his way over to Dilber, laughed heartily at the flower chaplet adorning her head and said: 'Come on Cleopatra, let's go!' Poor Cleopatra, she was the captive of this Alexander who dragged her against her will to the courtyard. Celal had already planned a pose for her that day. He would have her lean her back against a marble column and put on her a dress that had been patched in many places; torn and ripped near her arms and breasts. That's how he wanted to paint her. But Dilber refused: 'No! No! There is no way I will wear this', she told Celal Bey while holding the collars of her garment tightly with both hands. [...] Celal pressed his hands – strong enough to break any plaything – on Dilber's shoulders and dressed her up against her will. He then went to his corner and began a dramatic painting of a beggar girl. [...] Dilber had failed to defend herself. She leaned her head against the ancient column, feeling powerless and weak and wept softly. [...] One minute... Three minutes... Six minutes... Dilber was still crying. She felt so conscious of her slavery and so deeply humiliated by it. It was her slavery which had delivered her to the endless caprices of those who had prosperity and wealth, leaving her sad and heartbroken (p. 78).

The epiphany in this scene is twofold: Dilber understands how she is seen, and Celal sees Dilber beyond the fair Circassian trope. This realisation, Celal's acute grasp on who Dilber really is, has a profound effect on the reader as well. Dilber, enslaved in Celal's house, forced to be his model, represents an artistic trope that she does not embody, cries and expresses her dissent and embarrassment with her subservience. After this encounter, not only does Celal fall in love with Dilber, but he also vehemently opposes slavery.

The second important point about beauty and the Circassian trope is that Dilber enters the story as a child, not as a woman, and her character, in terms of the stamina that she shows to escape from slavery, supersedes her physical traits in the novel. Dilber's self-consciousness of her slavery, her inherent dignity and her longing for her mother's affection and homeland underscore her rebellion against her captivity throughout the novel. This is quite a deliberate portrayal of character over beauty by the writer, and it makes Dilber a heroine rather than a victim. In fact, the novel's ending, the iconic final line of the novel, 'to her freedom', sums up the tenor of Dilber's life as a slave: determined to defy her destiny as a slave, she walks into the waters of the Nile.

Political Struggles: Censorship, Exile and Legacy

The Adventures of a Slave Girl is Sezai's only novel, yet its literary influence extended beyond his own generation. The novel marked a turning point in Ottoman literature and continued to resonate with later writers and critics. Its publication was met with widespread enthusiasm, reinforcing its significance as a foundational text in the evolving landscape of Tanzimat literature. The novel's impact was immediate. Süleyman Nazif (1870–1927), a poet and prominent member of Committee of Union and Progress, recounted in his 1908 article 'On *The Adventures of a Slave Girl*', published in *Demet*, how upon its publication literature enthusiasts had rushed to the Bab-ı Ali, the publishing industry's centre of Istanbul, eager to obtain a copy. He described how Sezai's work shaped the emotions and perceptions of a generation.[26] Likewise, writers of the later period, particularly those of the *Edebiyat-ı Cedid* (New Literature Group), including Mehmet Rauf (1875–1931) and Tevfik Fikret (1867–1915), praised *The Adventures of a Slave Girl* as one of the earliest examples of literary storytelling in Ottoman literature.[27] In the Republican era, literary critics and historians read Sezai's novel with a myopic lens, either as a trail-blazing novel or failed attempt at realism, thus unable to recognize the authenticity of Sezai's fiction writing.

However, Sezai's novel challenged prevailing cultural and social norms by exposing both western exoticisation and the complicity of Ottoman intellectuals in perpetuating these narratives. This critical stance did not go unnoticed by the Hamidian regime. *The Adventures of a Slave Girl*, despite its literary merits, was viewed as politically subversive in its time, particularly for its implicit critique of bondage and its broader themes of personal freedom. As Sezai's own introduction makes clear,

[26] Süleyman Nazif, '*Sergüzeşt*'e Dair'.
[27] Mehmet Rauf, 'Romanlara Dair I, Bizde Hikaye'; Tevfik Fikret, 'Sami Paşazade Sezai Bey'.

The Adventures of a Slave Girl was considered politically controversial by the iron-fisted Hamidian regime of the time. During this oppressive era, the print press was under imperial scrutiny and suffocating censorship. Particularly, words pertaining to freedom and liberty were prohibited, and writers walked a thin line between exile and imprisonment. Writers, Sezai included, had to improvise creative ways to either bypass the censors or auto-censored their own texts. In a 1934 letter to Dr Besim Ömer Pasha, who translated the novel into French as *Dilber, La Biographie d'une esclave et l'eunuque amoureux* (The Biography of a Slave Girl and the Eunuch in Love), Sezai explained that the original title of the novel was *Bir Esirin Sergüzeşti* (Adventures of a Slave). However, for the Censorship Commission, even the word 'slave' was too provocative, and thus they removed it from the title before the publication.[28] The novel's implicit critique of bondage and the call for personal freedom drew unwanted attention from the palace, placing Sezai under surveillance.

In a 1926 interview with Mehmed Selahaddin for the journal *Yeni Kitab*, Sezai recalled how Yıldız Palace officials were unsettled by his references to liberty:

> The members of the palace did not appreciate my mention of freedom in my book. Whenever they had the opportunity, they did not hesitate to reprimand me. 'Speaking of liberty', they would say, 'does such behaviour, contrary to the loyalty expected of you, befit the scion of such an old family?'

The scrutiny went beyond verbal reprimands. Sezai was placed under constant surveillance, with undercover detectives tracking his movements. In his 1924 preface to the novel, he described the atmosphere that he had to endure:

> I was suffocated by the crushing, raging and ruinous restlessness of the times. Whenever I sat at my desk for the muse to honour and grace my poems, I would hear the footsteps of spies at my door, their predatory, tiger-like eyes watching through my window. For I had started *The Adventures of a Slave Girl* in opposition to slavery and concluded it with 'to her freedom' (p. 29).

Feeling increasingly stifled, Sezai left Istanbul in 1901 and sought refuge in Paris, where he joined the Young Turks. He remained in exile until the proclamation of the Second Constitution in 1908.

However, exile did not dampen Sezai's commitment to the ideals of freedom, a cause deeply rooted in his intellectual formation since the age of fourteen. One Turkish intellectual stands out in his early life as a

[28] This letter is referenced in the sole comprehensive monograph on the writer, Güven's *Sami Paşazade Sezayi ve Eserleri*.

formative figure. The young Sezai, who was radically influenced by the early Tanzimat writer Namık Kemal's ideas of freedom and patriotism, formed a life-long friendship with Kemal. Their first meeting in person took place in 1877, when Sezai was seventeen, during Kemal's imprisonment at the Sultanahmet General Prison. Sezai became Namık Kemal's most frequent visitor. Through their correspondence, Namık Kemal introduced him to European literature, particularly the works of Victor Hugo, whom he deeply admired and who influenced him greatly.[29]

Sezai remained true to Namık Kemal's ideological tone, particularly in his engagement with the concept of freedom, broadening the notion of freedom to encompass personal autonomy. Primarily through Dilber's struggle against enslavement, and to some extent through the constraints imposed on young people in matters of marriage, Sezai explored the boundaries of individual freedom within an empire grappling with modernity. His portrayal of both literal bondage and societal restrictions on personal choice reflects a broader critique of the limitations of freedom in Ottoman society.

This connection to Kemal is further reinforced through Sezai's deliberate references. His original title, *Bir Esirin Sergüzeşti* (The Adventures of a Slave), directly echoes Namık Kemal's *Sergüzeşt-i Ali Bey* (The Adventure of Ali Bey). Another unmistakable homage appears in the novel's final words, where the narrator concludes Dilber's story with '*hürriyetine*' (to her freedom). Ending his novel with the term '*hürriyet*', which Namık Kemal and other early Tanzimat writers had popularised and fought for, despite enduring exile and imprisonment as a consequence, during the Hamidian regime is a poignant tribute.

Like many of his contemporaries among the Tanzimat intellectuals, Sezai was not only a writer but also a government official, with a career in state service that spanned decades. In 1879, Samipaşazade Sezai began working at the Imperial Correspondence Office before serving as a clerk at the London Embassy from 1881 to 1885. The years following his return from London until his departure for Paris in 1901 marked his most productive period as a writer. However, this period was also fraught with loss and political tension. Sezai mourned the death of his mother, of Namık Kemal and of two siblings, while the empire suffered under the increasingly repressive rule of Abdülhamid II. This challenging period helped him forge important connections that later benefited him in Paris, where he joined the Young Turks and became the editor of the Committee of Union and Progress's publication, *Şûrâ-yı Ümmet*, in which he wrote

[29] Ibid., 40–41.

articles critiquing Ottoman state policies. After the proclamation of the Second Constitution in 1908, he returned to Istanbul and served as ambassador to Madrid from 1909 to 1921. Upon resigning in 1921, he wrote for various newspapers and magazines in Istanbul, until 1927, when the Turkish Parliament granted him a modest pension. He spent his final years in difficult financial circumstances, living in a house in Kadıköy, which the Istanbul Municipality rented for him, and there he passed away on 26 April 1936.

Unlike many Tanzimat novels, some of which have been long forgotten and obscured by the alphabet reform of 1928, *The Adventures of a Slave Girl* has enjoyed an enduring legacy and retained its relevance until the present day. Today, Sezai's short-story collection *Küçük Şeyler* (Little Things) and *The Adventures of a Slave Girl* are required readings in Turkish high school curricula, and more than fifty editions of the novel are in circulation, making Sezai one of the most widely read Ottoman writers in modern Turkey. What makes his writing and life relevant, even after a century and a half, is his unflinching dedication to capturing the human condition, especially the silent tragedies that often go unnoticed. His characters inhabit an empire immersed in an angst of westernisation and socio-cultural reform, but for Sezai it is the individual – broken, yearning and defiant – who rises above the tide of history to demand her freedom and dignity.

Burcu Karahan and İclal Vanwesenbeeck

Works Cited

Ahmet Mithat. *Felâtun Bey and Râkim Efendi: An Ottoman Novel.* Translated by Melih Levi and Monica M. Ringer, Syracuse University Press, 2016.

Beecher Stowe, Harriet. *Uncle Tom's Cabin.* Penguin Classics, 1981.

Bertram, Carel. *Imagining the Turkish House: Collective Visions of Home.* University of Texas Press, 2008.

Fatma Aliye. 'Women of Islam'. Translated by Gregory Key. Translation Attached Publishing House, 2026.

Tevfik Fikret. 'Sami Paşazade Bey'. *Servet-i Fünun*, vol. 15, no. 382, 1898, p. 2.

Gürbilek, Nurdan. 'Dandies and Originals: Authenticity, Belatedness, and the Turkish Novel'. *The South Atlantic Quarterly*, vol. 102, nos 2/3, 2003, pp. 599–628.

Güven, Güler. *Sami Paşazade Sezayi ve Eserleri.* Dergâh Yayınları, 2009.

Kandiyoti, Deniz. 'Slave Girls, Temptresses, and Comrades: Images of Women in Turkish Novel'. *Feminist Issues*, vol. 8, no. 1, 1988, pp. 35–50.

Kaplan, Mehmet, et al., editors. *Yeni Türk Edebiyatı Antolojisi, 1865–1876.* Vol. II. Marmara Üniversitesi Fen Edebiyat Fakültesi, 1993.

Mehmet Rauf. 'Romanlara Dair I, Bizde Hikaye'. *Servet-i Fünun*, vol. 14, no. 344, 1897, pp. 6–7.
Mümtaz, Semih. *Tarihimizde Hayal Olmuş Hakikatler.* Hilmi Kitabevi, 1948.
Özgül, M. Kayahan. *Yenişehirli Avni: Hayatı ve Eserleri.* Kültür Bakanlığı Yayınları, 1990.
Sami Moralı, Seniha. 'Türk Kültürüne Büyük Hizmetleri Dokunan bir Devlet Adamı: Subhi Paşa'. *Hayat Tarih*, vol. 2, no. 11, 1968, pp. 69–74.
Samipaşazade Sezai. 'Küçük Şeyler'. *Bütün Eserleri: Tıpkıbasım*, edited by Zeynep Kerman, Türk Dil Kurumu Yayınları, 2017, pp. 99–141.
Süleyman Nazif. '*Sergüzeşt*'e Dair'. *Demet*, vol. 3, 1 Teşrin-i Evvel 1324 / 14 Aralık 1908, pp. 39–40.
Parla, Jale. *Babalar ve Oğullar: Tanzimat Romanının Epistemolojik Temelleri.* İletişim Yayınları, 1990.
Parlatır, İsmail. *Tanzimat Edebiyatında Kölelik.* Türk Tarih Kurumu Basımevi, 1992.
Tanpınar, Ahmet Hamdi. *XIX. Asır Türk Edebiyatı Tarihi*, edited by Abdullah Uçman, Yapı Kredi Yayınları, 2006.
Tevfik Fikret. 'Sami Paşazade Sezai Bey'. *Servet-i Fünun*, vol. 15, no. 382, 1898, p. 2.
Topal, Alp Eren, and Selim Karlıtekin, editors. *Sürgünde Muhalefet: Namık Kemal'in Hürriyet Gazetesi: Tüm Koleksiyon.* VakıfBank Kültür Yayınları, 2018.
Uslu, Mehmet Fatih, and Fatih Altuğ, editors. *Tanzimat ve Edebiyat: Osmanlı İstanbul'unda Modern Edebi Kültür.* Türkiye İş Bankası, 2014.

Figure 2 Committee of Young Turks. Samipaşazade Sezai (top right, back) with the Young Turks, 1909. Courtesy of IBB Atatürk Library.

Samipaşazade Sezai's 1924 Preface to *The Adventures of a Slave Girl*[1]

When *The Adventures of a Slave Girl* came out in 1888, it was exceptionally well-received by the young people who had already started to enlighten the future. *The Adventures of a Slave Girl* guided those young people, my contemporaries, those enlightened minds and relentless intellectual pioneers, gaining popularity day after day, as you, Sezai, withdrew from public view. Considering this enthusiastic reception of the novel by intellectual circles, you should have written five or ten more books after *The Adventures of a Slave Girl*. That book was a promise. Why did you not keep your promise, Sezai?

In 1888, the Ottoman Empire had been in a thirty-three-year-long night with no hope of dawn, not a glimmer of light on the horizon. The few stars that appeared in the sky during this prolonged darkness had left their homeland, vanishing into the horizons of distant, foreign lands. Those who remained behind briefly flickered in the homeland's sky before being engulfed by the black fog rising from the volcanoes of *istibdad*.[2] During that period, the natural course of intellectual life was disrupted by ideological conflict and inner turmoil, spreading from individuals to society, from society to nations, and from nations to the entire homeland. There was

1 Samipaşazade Sezai wrote this preface to the second edition of his *The Adventures of a Slave Girl* in 1924, thirty-six years after the novel's original publication in 1888 by the publishing house Kitaphane-i Sudi. By the time of the second publication, the Ottoman Empire had been dissolved, and modern Turkey had just emerged as a republic. In that sense, this introduction serves as a retrospective reflection on the repressive Hamidian era, during which the novel was originally written.

2 The period starting with the end of the First Constitutional Era on 13 February 1878 and ending with the proclamation of the Second Constitutional Era on 23 July 1908 is usually referred to by the term *istibdad*, meaning oppression, despotism, tyranny and dictatorship, defining the reign of Sultan Abdülhamid II (1876–1909).

no peaceful corner left in the entire homeland where one could immerse oneself in literature. These events affected me as well. I was suffocated by the crushing, raging and ruinous restlessness of the times. Whenever I sat at my desk for the muse to honour and grace my poems, I would hear the footsteps of spies at my door, their predatory, tiger-like eyes watching through my window. For I had started *The Adventures of a Slave Girl* in opposition to slavery and concluded it with 'to her freedom'.

In those days, elsewhere in the world, the floating palaces of other nations traversed the oceans for prosperity and trade, the exchange of information, knowledge and innovations, connecting continents, even reaching the poles in pursuit of scientific breakthroughs, and here, in Istanbul, we were forbidden from crossing from one shore of the Bosphorus to the other at night. Yet those shores were the world's most beautiful soft cushions made of flowers, for daydreaming in the already heavenly Bosphorus.

To describe my state of mind at the time, thirty-five years ago I wrote a few lines:

> See, no power left to bide, might has flown
> In a corner of solitude, I've grown old alone
> My hope still rests in my homeland's destiny,
> But, shattered, it lies in the foe's zone
> Each day I witness in this land of mine
> A state of anguish with sighing, crying and moaning
> I stood firm against both favour and threat,
> With courage and zeal I made it my own

I no longer remember the rest of this rather long poem. But I was not deterred, and I kept writing. After I had published *Küçük Şeyler* (Little Things)[3]and *Rumûzü'l-Edeb* (Secrets of Literature),[4] I moved to Paris and continued my fight through the newspaper *Şûrâ-yı Ümmet* (Council of the People).[5] If all that I wrote in that newspaper and elsewhere were

[3] *Küçük Şeyler* (Little Things) is the title of Samipaşazade Sezai's short-story collection published in 1891.

[4] This title, *Rumûzü'l-Edeb* (Secrets of Literature), is a reference to *Rumûzü'l-Hikem* (Secrets of Wisdom), a work authored by Sezai's father, Abdurrahman Sami Pasha (1792–1881), and published in 1871. It focuses on faith, morality and Sufism.

[5] *Şûrâ-yı Ümmet* was one of the official media outlets of the Committee of Union and Progress (CUP). It was published between 1902 and 1910 in Cairo, Paris, Istanbul and Thessaloniki, playing a significant role in the 1908 Young Turk Revolution. On 20 July 1906, Samipaşazade Sezai was appointed editor-in-chief, and from issue 98 (published on 15 August 19906) onwards, the newspaper became the official publication of the CUP.

compiled, it would yield several volumes akin to *The Adventures of a Slave Girl*.[6] However, my intention is not to bring to these pages the fury and havoc of the past. I obviously write about the past to show that the environment in which an author lives and the influences and sorrows that surround him have an undeniable effect on what he writes – or, more importantly, what he is unable to write.

In those days, it was difficult to find topics for novels similar to those of Europeans. But then why write like Europeans? There were countless ordinary and authentic topics for novels. Besides, I cannot write about something I haven't experienced – more precisely, I wouldn't wish to write about it. Yet, masterpieces are written more with reason than with emotion, for works that are dominated by emotion tend to become effeminate. For instance, in the captivating architecture of the Arabs in Andalusia, emotion has prevailed so overwhelmingly that their hearts are visible on the stone walls, and the colours of their magnificent palace decorations come from the tears and smiles of their dreams. The Arabs, who immersed themselves in the intoxicating vision of poetry that only noble souls and such a refined civilisation could perceive, could not achieve immortality among the harsh Spaniards of that time, among the people whom my great poet Saadi described as such:

> All men are the children of Adam,
> Yet they spill each other's blood like wolves[7]

They would be compelled to abandon Andalusia. Their noble art in Andalusia conveys this truth to all who can understand its language.

On the other hand, in the fine arts of the Romans, the greatest and most ruthless nation in the world, emotion seems almost absent. The marble columns that seem as if they could carry the entire sky are each an idea, a thought. Their mighty palaces with their marble columns and marble staircases, turning crimson at sunset, stand as triumphal

[6] All of Sezai's articles for the newspaper *Şûrâ-yı Ümmet* have been compiled and published by Zeynep Kerman in his collected works. Samipaşazade Sezai, *Bütün Eserleri II*.

[7] This couplet is taken from the Persian poet Saadi of Shiraz's (1210–91/92) masterpiece *Gulistan*, which Sezai and Abdülhak Hamit Tarhan studied with Sezai's father, Sami Pasha.

arches against eternity, like the works of Namık Kemal[8] and Süleyman Nazif[9]...

Thus, in Namık Kemal's style, there is a mighty quality inherited from his ancestors. I would like to use Namık Kemal's own words to describe what he represents in Turkish literature and political life. While visiting the coast of Great Britain, Kemal described England by saying (although this description is not literal, its meaning remains true): 'It could be said that every time the tides rise, all the world's needs flow from England to the globe, and as the tides recede, the treasures and wealth of the world pour back onto the island'.[10] In my view, Namık Kemal himself is the same. The essence in Kemal is that, when he is at high tide, all the materials and needs of the Turkish mind and soul flow from that wellspring of genius. At low tide, all the treasures and gems of inspiration pour back to his world of knowledge. The ebb of that meaning and understanding has perfected many pearls, one of which is Süleyman Nazif. Carrying all the fire of his people in his heart and his eastern sun-forged style in his pen, he, too, stands as guard at the Turkish frontiers of knowledge, steadfast against any violations and beyond fleeting literary movements.

I wanted to honour Ekrem, our sentimental master, by dedicating *The Adventures of a Slave Girl* to his eternal heart.[11] If this work has any merit,

[8] Namık Kemal, an Ottoman writer, intellectual, reformer, journalist, playwright and political activist, played a pivotal role in shaping the new westernised Ottoman literature and the ideology of the Young Ottomans and Turkish nationalist movements. He is especially renowned for advocating the ideals of freedom and homeland through his impassioned patriotic plays and poems, notably *The Motherland or Silistre*. As a first-generation Tanzimat writer, he was influential on the subsequent generation of writers, including Sezai.

[9] Süleyman Nazif (1869–1927) was a Kurdish Ottoman journalist and poet of the *Servet-i Fünun* era, a political activist in the Second Constitutional Period, as well as the governor of several cities in the Ottoman Empire, including Baghdad. He wrote numerous articles and books, as well as a poetry collection titled *Malta Nights* about his two-year exile in Malta.

[10] Here, Sezai is referencing Namık Kemal's article 'Terakki', published in the newspaper *İbret*; *İbret*, no. 45, 4 November 1872, pp. 1–3. In this article, Namık Kemal has said: 'If one were to visit the warehouses along the banks of the Thames River and observe the daily imports and exports, one might say that the tides, which cause the river to rise and fall once a day, bring all the products of the world here and from here, disperse all the goods that mankind produces' (*Thames Nehri'nin kenarında olan mahzenlere gidilse de her gün vukû bulan ithalat ve ihracata bakılsa adem der ki; nehrin günde bir kere yükselip bir kere alçalmasını mucip olan cezr ü med ile dünyanın ne kadar mahsulatı var ise buraya dökülüp geliyor, insanın ne kadar mamulatı varsa buradan dağılıp gidiyor*).

[11] Sezai dedicated the first edition of his 1888 novel to Recaizade Mahmud Ekrem, a close friend and one of the most influential second-generation Tanzimat writers. Ekrem's only

Figure 3 Lunch at Mithat Cemal Kuntay's flat at the Mısır Apartment. Courtesy of Kapı Yayınları.

it has drawn it from that very heart, which, though buried in the bosom of the earth, now will forever beat in undying greatness.

Samipaşazade Sezai
Vaniköy, 4 March 1924

Note: This photograph – first featured in Mithat Cemal Kuntay's 1939 book on the renowned poet Mehmet Akif Ersoy, titled *Mehmet Âkif Ersoy: Hayatı, Seciyesi, Sanatı* (Mehmet Akif Ersoy: His Life, Character and Art) – was taken in 1924 in Kuntay's flat in the Mısır Apartment on İstiklal Street in the Beyoğlu district, during a lunch gathering with prominent writers of the time to celebrate the publication of Ersoy's book *Asım*. The guests, from left to right are, Cenap Şahabettin, Abdülhak Hamit Tarhan, Süleyman Nazif, Ersoy's son Emin Akif, Mehmet Akif Ersoy and Samipaşazade Sezai. The host, Mithat Cemal Kuntay, is standing behind Ersoy and his son. Beşir Ayvazoğlu has written an entire book about this

novel, *Araba Sevdası* (The Carriage Affair, 1889), is considered the first realist novel in Ottoman literature. Its protagonist, the *alafranga* dandy Bihruz Bey, became an iconic character, inspiring Şerif Mardin to coin the term 'Bihruz Bey syndrome'. See Mardin, 'Super Westernization in Urban Life in the Ottoman Empire', pp. 412–13.

photograph, titled *1924 bir Fotoğrafin Uzun Hikayesi* (The Long Story of a 1924 Photograph, 2023) and has speculated that, although they had gathered to celebrate Ersoy's *Asım*, Sezai must have brought copies of *The Adventures of a Slave Girl* to his friends, as the novel's second edition had just come out before this gathering. What is more striking than the prominent line of guests in this photograph are the two domestic slave women in the background, photographed but unnamed, subtly blending into the salon's décor, their presence a sign of status. Positioned on either side of Tarhan, a life-long friend of Sezai, whose mother was also a slave, these women appear, perhaps deceptively, to have posed for the portrait. Yet these women, who had most certainly prepared the elaborate table setting and now stand ready to serve, are stark reminders of the lingering realities of female slavery and servitude well into the early years of the Republic – just as *The Adventures of a Slave Girl* saw its second edition. It is important to remember that slavery was not fully abolished in the Republic until 1964, despite Turkey ratifying the 1926 League of Nations Convention on the Suppression of Slavery in 1933 (see Erdem, *Slavery in the Ottoman Empire*, p. xix).

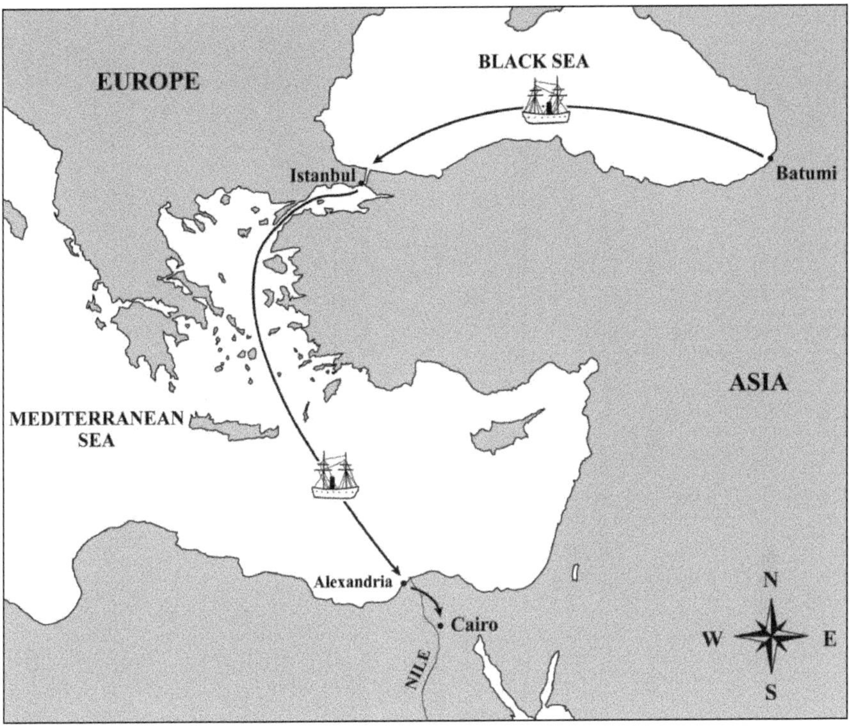

Figure 4 Map of Dilber's journey as a Circassian slave. Illustrated by Gaosheng Yang.

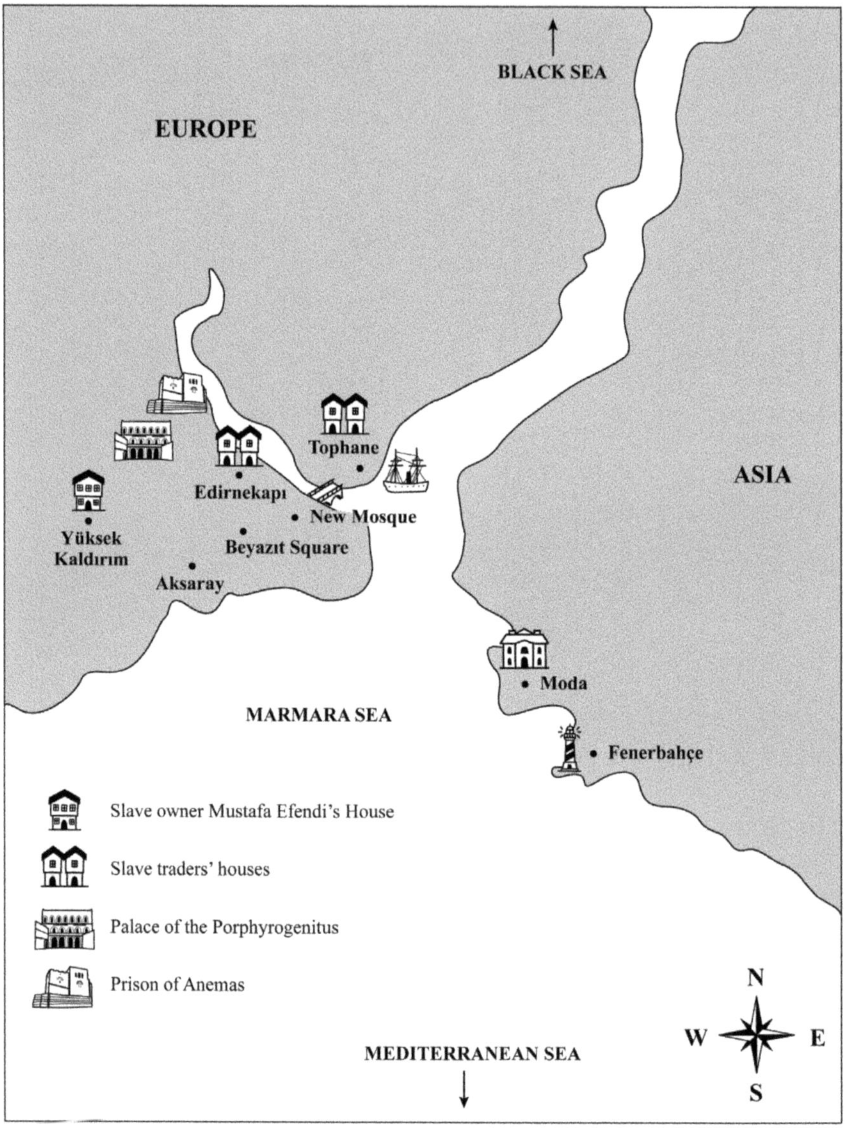

Figure 5 Map of Greater Istanbul with locations mentioned in the novel. Illustrated by Gaosheng Yang.

THE ADVENTURES OF A SLAVE GIRL

Figure 6 Tophane Harbour in Istanbul. Courtesy of IBB Atatürk Library.

The Adventures of a Slave Girl

Chapter 1

When one of the Russian steamboats from Batum approached Tophane,[1] the few men waiting anxiously on their small rowboats jumped right over onto it. Once on the steamboat, one of them started talking to a tall, broad-shouldered Circassian[2] who had a thin, black moustache and was wearing a long Circassian coat,[3] tightly buttoned around his waist. He was holding his traditional calpac[4] in one hand and a silver whip in the other.

'It's good to see you', the man said. 'Where are the slave girls?'

'Right here'.

'How many?'

'Three'.

'Are they pretty?'

Flaunting one of the slaves, the Circassian said: 'Look at those blue eyes. A pasha would pay a fortune for these eyes'.

The Circassian and the man climbed into one boat, the slave girls were stacked onto another, and all set sail towards Tophane Harbour. The rather burly man beside the Circassian was a slave trader named Hajji Ömer. Selling people had turned his cold heart to stone, and you could see the reflection of that savage heart in his tiger-like gaze. Despite being, broadly speaking, human himself, Hajji Ömer remained indifferent to any

[1] A district in Istanbul where the city's port was located and many slave traders resided. It was often referred to as the slave neighbourhood or district. This was the final destination for slaves who were brought to Istanbul by sea.

[2] In the nineteenth-century Ottoman Empire, the terms 'Circassian' and 'Caucasian' were used interchangeably as umbrella terms for all North Caucasian Muslims.

[3] A traditional, collarless, caftan-like wool topcoat with a tight waistline and buttons, worn by Circassians.

[4] A traditional, high-crowned cap made of animal skin, felt, or other material, worn by Circassian men.

human tragedy, unless it served his selfish purposes. To him, there was no difference between a girl's songs and sobs, nor between the tunes of a lute and the desperate pleas of a remarkable beauty. He held only two things sacred in life: the force behind his trade – his whip – and the poor, abandoned girls who came into his house.

On the boat, Hajji Ömer was busy bargaining over the slave girls. His big, round eyes were fixed on the Circassian, while his big hands moved like two fans. If for some reason the bargaining didn't go his way, the deep wrinkles and the dirty-looking grey beard (which made him look like he was in his forties or fifties) on his dark countenance transformed him into a repugnant beast.

As for the slave girls, the two older ones appeared to be around sixteen or seventeen, both dazzling Caucasian jewels. The third was a young slave girl, likely eight or nine years old. Her narrow forehead, rather tiny mouth, small waist, rounded shoulders and especially the spark of wisdom in her black eyes exuded a boundless grace. She was like a painting sketched by a masterful hand and still waiting to be coloured. Her miniature lips were rather pale, her hair had thinned out from neglect, her face was pallid from destitution and the recent arduous voyage, and there were dark circles around her eyes. In her gaze was the hidden sorrow and sadness of a caged bird that looked up at the heavens. The little girl was clad in a tight Circassian coat buttoned all the way down, and on her head was her old small calpac.

Once the rowboats had reached Tophane Harbour, the slave girls were taken to a house where the wife of the slave trader greeted them.

'These two look pretty', she pointed at the older slave girls, 'but this little one seems sickly. Did you bring her here to die?' she asked her husband.

'So, what?', Hajji Ömer replied. 'It's not as if we paid a thousand liras for her, is it? She is exactly the kind of youngling that Mustafa Efendi's wife in the Yüksek Kaldırım neighbourhood asked for'.[5]

That night, the Circassian man stayed in Hajji Ömer's house, and by the next morning they had completed the bargaining. All three girls were sold on the condition that they could be returned within three days.

In Hajji Ömer's house, the slave girls would gather in one room in the evenings and talk to each other. However, laughing too much and speaking Circassian were forbidden, and if a girl was returned by a customer, for whatever reason, she would receive ten to fifteen lashes.

[5] A neighbourhood in the Fatih district of Istanbul.

One morning, a few weeks after their arrival at this house, Hajji Ömer said: 'Come on, we are leaving', in Circassian, speaking to the little slave girl in her native language.

She immediately rose from her seat and, like any child her age, ran to one of the girls with whom she had travelled, wrapping her arms around her. When they finally kissed goodbye, tears welled up in her eyes, revealing the suffering in her young soul. Then, like those who suddenly begin to feel the heavy burden of life on their shoulders, she furrowed her tiny brows, with a solemn, deep and contemplative expression took the slave trader's big hand and stepped outside the house. They walked on.

As they walked down the street, the child watched the cars and the tram in awe. When they arrived at Tophane Square, she noticed a group of children frolicking and laughing joyfully.

Like all children who go after their heart's desire without a second thought, she ran up to them in ecstasy, eager to join them like birds in the sky join their flock. But suddenly, the slave trader's big, dreadful eyes sprang open. 'Come back here', he yelled at her, 'or I'll take the whip out'. As soon as she heard those words, the child slowly and unwillingly turned back. And as she grasped the hand of this ghoul once again, she felt, for the first time, the full weight of her bondage in his ironclad claws.

They walked on. Neither of them uttered a word. On the Galata Bridge, her eyes were fixed on the steamboats, docking and departing on either side of the bridge.[6] After a few more steps, the instant the sound of a steamer's whistle reached her, a shiver seized her entire body, for the echo of a steamer's whistle in Batum, which had taken her from her homeland, still lingered in her memory. A breeze blowing from the mountains that stood shoulder to shoulder on the horizon, beneath a blue sky, swept across her hair, reminding her of a dream she had once had – a dream of her homeland – offering her aching heart a strange solace.

They walked on. When they crossed the Galata Bridge and arrived in front of the New Mosque, the child lifted her utterly pallid face in fear and hesitation. 'I am hungry', she murmured in Circassian. The slave trader

[6] Galata, located at the entrance of the Golden Horn, is a vital crossing point connecting 'the old city' to the Pera district. In the late nineteenth century, three different bridges were built at this location. The first, a wooden pontoon bridge known as *Cisr-i Cedid* (the New Bridge), was constructed in 1845. It was replaced in 1863 by another wooden pontoon bridge, built in anticipation of Napoleon III's visit to Istanbul. The third Galata Bridge, in use from 1875 to 1912, was an iron pontoon bridge, measuring 480 metres in length and 14 metres in width. Although *Adventures of a Slave Girl* was published in 1881, during the period when the third bridge was in use, the narrative timeline requires that Dilber and Hajji Ömer must cross the Golden Horn on the second Galata Bridge.

Figure 7 Galata Bridge in Istanbul. Courtesy of IBB Atatürk Library.

grabbed her by the arm and pulled her so roughly that the child nearly fell, but he pushed her up again and snapped: 'Walk!'

They walked on. The poor child's pale yet beautiful lips trembled. As they walked up the Çakmakçılar Hill, she could feel her feet aching but was too afraid to speak up. The ten-pace stretch ahead of them seemed like an endless expanse, a distance that no amount of walking could conquer. She struggled to walk upright, and her feet got tangled, causing her to lose her balance once again. Yet she managed to stand on her feet and take another step forward.

They walked on. By the time they had reached Beyazıt Square, the girl could no longer lift her eyes and look around, and since her legs felt like two sticks of lead tied to her body, she had to muster all her strength to drag them. Thank goodness, they finally stopped at a coffee house near the Beyazıt tram station. To the exhausted child, that wicker stool offered peace and joy as sublime as a queen's ascent to her throne. The slave trader purchased a *simit* and some cheese. After the child devoured them and had a glass of water, they took the tram to Aksaray. From there, they caught another tram and finally reached the Yüksek Kaldırım neighbourhood.

The slave trader and the child finally arrived at a secluded street in a quiet neighbourhood. It was noontime, and the eastern sun illuminated this small, secluded street with its radiant beams. The slave trader stopped

Figure 8 Beyazıt Square in Istanbul. Courtesy of IBB Atatürk Library.

in front of a house and knocked on the door. The upper windows of the house were overshadowed by the eaves, while the rays seeping through the lattices of the lower windows seemed to dim as they spread inside. All of a sudden, a blind beggar appeared from around the corner, tapping his cane on the sidewalk, keeping the rhythm and singing: 'When I have your ruby lips to sip, I don't surrender to the rose-coloured wine'.[7] There was a dog sleeping at the door of the house, and a few cats prowled on the neighbour's roof. The architecture and the stillness of these streets could easily make you think you were travelling back to the Middle Ages.

An Arab slave girl opened the door.[8] 'Welcome, Hajji Ömer Efendi, come in', she said. After informing her mistress of their arrival, she returned to lead the child and the slave trader to her mistress's room. The mistress, a fat and dark-skinned woman, was sitting in the corner, her head

[7] This couplet is from a popular ghazal of the time, attributed to Osman Nevres, a nineteenth-century Ottoman lyric poet, also known by his pen name Nevres-i Cedid or Nevres Efendi, a regular at Sezai's father's mansion. The ghazal was set to music by Hacı Faik Bey, a prominent composer from Istanbul, known for his contributions to both religious and secular music. It was composed in the Tahir-Buselik mode: '*Devr-i la'linde baş eğmem bade-i gül-fama ben*'.

[8] In the Ottoman Empire, African slaves were often called 'Arab' due to linguistic, geographic and cultural associations rather than accurate ethnic classification.

wrapped in a headscarf, her brows thickly smeared with kohl: an uncouth soul in an ugly guise.

As soon as they entered the mistress's room, the slave trader ordered the little girl: 'Go ahead, kiss the hem of your mistress's garment'. But when the little slave wanted to embrace her instead, the woman pushed her away rather firmly. Dispirited, the little slave stepped back and sat on the floor cushion.

'How dare you sit on a floor cushion? You are a slave! Up on your feet!' Hajji Ömer bellowed, enraged. Turning to the mistress, he quickly apologised. 'Please excuse her', he said. 'She's not trained yet. She only arrived a few days ago. You can discipline her however you see fit'.

Sad and confused, the child obeyed all their orders. First, the mistress patted down every inch of her body and found many defects. Of course, these were just petty excuses to lower her price. Then, the Arab slave girl conducted her own thorough examination and said:

'Ma'am, she is useless. Too skinny. She won't survive'.

Their greedy and selfish bargaining over how to exploit a human being lasted for hours before they finally settled on forty liras as the sale price for the slave girl.

> This contract hereby is to declare that I have sold a slave of Circassian origin, aged nine, free of any illness or defect, for the sum of forty Ottoman liras to the wife of Mustafa Efendi, former Fiscal Director of Harput. The deed is written and handed over to the afore-mentioned lady to certify the transaction.
>
> Slave Trader Hajji Ömer

Thanks to his acquired expertise, Hajji Ömer was able to swiftly pen this deed and leave the house.

Following her mistress's orders, the Arab slave girl took the quiet and obedient little slave girl down to the kitchen. She made her carry water while she herself started cooking. The mistress was very particular about how she ran the house and maintained its order meticulously. She always yelled at everyone and lost her temper very quickly. The mistress's dull, black, glaring eyes harboured enough cruelty to reduce a child to tears and even frighten a grown man. Strangely, it was only when she embraced her twelve-year-old daughter, Atiye, that she showed any sign of kindness and compassion. These feminine virtues seemed to be reserved solely for her daughter, for otherwise she disliked children and showed pity to no one.

Chapter 1

In her youth, the mistress had occasionally been subjected to her husband's brutal beatings and had suffered abundantly from feelings of jealousy, which can transform even the gentlest of women into a wild animal. And for a while now, she had been distressed about her husband's dismissal from his government post for bribery and corruption by a court order. In the end, these experiences had filled her heart with nothing but cruelty and gloom. And because she didn't have any intellectual curiosities, civility and good manners expected of any good mother in society, she would constantly pester the slave girls, beat them brutally and gossip about her neighbours.

As for her husband, he spent his days trying to clear his name from the embezzlement charges and get his government post back, coming home late every night and leaving at the break of dawn.

At nighttime, Taravet, the Arab slave girl, set down a rather thin mattress, a firm pillow and a filthy quilt for the little slave, who, exhausted from walking all day, crawled right into it. As she stared at the faint candlelight that reflected from the upper floor window onto the branches of the pomegranate tree in the yard, a mysterious sensation came over her. 'Nighttime', she whispered, then pulled the cover over her head and fell into a calm, deep and innocent sleep.

When she opened her eyes in the morning, a bird was chirping on the pomegranate tree. There is indeed such an affinity between a bird's song and a child's soul. The little slave rose from her bed, rested her head on the window and started watching the bird. As the bird flapped its wings towards the rising sun, the red, the blue and all other colours of dawn danced on its chest, making it resemble a newly blossomed flower on a tree. The little slave was so consumed by this spectacle that it was only the sound of Taravet's scolding – 'Come here and put your bed away' – that brought her back.

Taravet handed her a broom and showed her the rooms to sweep, the chores to do and the water to carry upstairs and to the kitchen. They named the little slave girl Dilber, simply because the mistress had started calling her by this name. Poor Dilber, she got up so early every morning and struggled to fold and tuck away her thin mattress. Then she swept the rooms and lugged buckets of water up the stairs.

One morning, while she was sweeping the rooms upstairs, Dilber saw Miss Atiye playing with her toys. Setting her broom aside, Dilber went to join her and started to look at the toys in awe. Suddenly she was startled by the mistress's horrific voice yelling: 'Dilber, Dilber!' Dilber froze. When the mistress walked in and saw that an ordinary slave girl was trying to play with her daughter, she grabbed Dilber by the ear and dragged her to the door where she had left her broom.

'How dare you leave your work and play?' she yelled and slapped her. Poor child! She did not even dare to cry as she went back to work.

Each morning, she laboured through her chores. The tiniest mistake would earn her a slap – either from the mistress or from Taravet. After completing her duties at home, she walked to school with Miss Atiye and returned in the afternoon, carrying the schoolbags.

As weeks and months passed, Dilber started to speak and understand Turkish with the remarkable skill that most children show in learning new languages. Yet it was evident in her sagging cheeks and dead eyes that life, which brought joy to her peers, was turning out to be nothing but hardship and suffering for her, for she was crushed under the weight of the morning duties and beaten brutally for brief moments of joy. Even though early on Miss Atiye had wanted to play with her, after seeing how her mother and Taravet treated Dilber, she too started to chase her away every time Dilber came near her, yelling: 'You filthy slave! Get out, go downstairs!'

In this miserable life of hers, which passed in sorrow and suffering, Dilber's only pleasure was to go to school. For only there could she talk to other children with the freedom and affection that she desperately needed. There, nobody crushed this little being's dignity by calling her a 'filthy slave'. On the contrary, despite her state of misery and suffering, she even received occasional praise from her teacher for doing her best. All of this was a cure for her broken heart. Moreover, at school she also found a dear friend, a little confidante named Miss Lütfiye. These two kindred spirits enjoyed each other's company so much that they soon became inseparable and shared everything with each other.

'Who's your owner?' asked Lütfiye one day.

'The mistress', said Dilber.

'Which mistress?'

Pointing to Miss Atiye, she said: 'Her mother'.

'Do you have toys?'

'No. I am a slave'.

'I'll give you a toy'.

After this brief conversation, Lütfiye took a baby doll from her bag and gave it to Dilber. Feeling extremely fortunate, Dilber accepted it with great joy and hid it in the bedroom closet. Dilber was so worried that the cruel Sudanese slave[9] Taravet would see her doll and shatter all her dreams that, whenever someone entered the room, she formed a habit of saying:

[9] In the nineteenth century, most enslaved people in the Ottoman Empire were African women primarily destined for domestic service; see Toledano's *The Ottoman Slave Trade and its Suppression, 1840–1890*.

'I don't have a thing in the closet!' From then on, every time Lütfiye gave her sweets and fruit, Dilber quickly hid them in her bag, among her schoolbooks. But one day Miss Atiye saw Dilber taking candy from Lütfiye and told her mother about it as soon as she returned home. Since the ongoing failure in her husband's state of affairs and the difficulties that she encountered in running the house had exacerbated her already angry demeanour and abiding misery, the mistress took her beloved daughter's complaint seriously. The truth was that this was nothing more than a display of childish arrogance and poor manners on Miss Atiye's part, yet the mistress still summoned Dilber to her room, already determined to punish her for her misdeed.

'Come over here, you nasty Circassian. Come here, you filthy beggar', she said.

When the child entered the room, the mistress opened her dull eyes wide and raised her kohl-smeared brows, and she kept repeating the words: 'Come here, I said!' Dilber was horror-stricken in a way only children can be. She froze and started shaking. The mistress rose to her feet, grabbed Dilber by the arm and mercilessly slapped her a few times. 'Now, do you see what happens to those who beg?' she asked, and with that she threw all the sweets and fruit from her bag out the window. That evil woman. She destroyed all that Dilber had, all the treasure she had in the world, without mercy.

Her miserable life had no doubt given the little slave girl's character a certain kind of calmness and resignation. And although her mistress's beating had deeply upset Dilber's already wounded soul, with a remarkable willpower, rarely seen in people of her age, she held back her tears. But alas, as she was about to leave the room, a few tears welled up in her sad eyes.

Before long, Taravet was calling this poor Caucasian from downstairs:

'You filthy Circassian, come over here and carry some water to the kitchen!'

The child followed her orders and fetched water from the garden well as the freezing rain kept falling on her from the black clouds that the strong northerly wind had carried in from the horizon. As the bucket swung back and forth in her hands and water droplets spilled on her, she felt the freezing cold right in her heart. After bringing the buckets into the kitchen, she had no courage left to go outside and no strength to carry more water. Taravet, busy with cooking, turned to her and said:

'Come on, lazybones, bring more water, otherwise dinner won't be ready'.

The child, unable to move, said: 'I cannot do it anymore'.

When Taravet heard this, she grabbed a piece of hot firewood from the hearth and walked towards Dilber. Her bloodshot eyes looked scary, like the eyes of a snake that was about to turn anyone into stone – a savage gaze that is peculiar to her kind of people. The child thought a volcano was erupting over her, or that the gatekeeper of hell was chasing her with a mace in his hand. The poor little slave got so rattled and scared that she immediately surrendered to Taravet's orders and went outside. Moaning and groaning, she finished the task, a task far beyond what her frail body could endure.

That night, when everyone was in a deep sleep and the wall clock struck midnight like an owl in a cemetery, Dilber got up from her bed. She opened the closet quietly and took something out. Then she rested her head on her hands and started to think with the tenacity of an army commander. How terrible! What was this child doing in the middle of a cold and dark night? Yes, she was going to escape… She was going to flee… But the black, majestic wings of the night that spread across the sky like a mythical giant cannot be a refuge for such a tiny creature. Yes, she was about to flee… Moved by a force unknown even to herself, her feet would guide her to go and seek something, perhaps a destination. She would perhaps find the only shelter for which she yearned, one that would fill the big hole in her heart. She would find her mother so that she could finally find solace and consolation, break free from this state of being forgotten and abandoned, and cry to her heart's content in her mother's loving embrace.

Poor slave! With a noble gesture, she took off the dress that her mistress had given her. She grabbed her Circassian coat and calpac from a dusty corner of the closet. While putting them on, she was anxiously eyeing her black omen, Taravet, who was sleeping in her bed. The light emanating from the candle, faint and feeble like the star of hope, cast a ghastly glow on the worn-out cardigan on the cushion, the tattered dress and on Taravet who lay in a deep, heavy sleep. For an escape of this kind one needed to pack things, she thought to herself. Then she untied the bundle in which she carried her schoolbooks. First and foremost, she put into it the doll that Lütfiye had given her. Then she placed an apple and, after that, her two metal rings. She was weeping quietly as she packed all she owned in this world. Well done to the tormented yet noble heart of this little Caucasian for leaving the room, carrying in her bundle nothing but her own belongings.

Dilber groped her way down the stairs in the dark. When she approached the main gate, however, she noticed that the door was bolted. This iron shield, this unbearable obstacle was in her way. She froze in grave despair.

Fired by her anguish and desperation, this little slave climbed on a stool and tried to push the bolt. Not possible! Though her hands were shaking with exasperation and dismay, she tried one more time. It was impossible! The iron bolt remained unmoved, just like the hearts of her mistress and Taravet. When she pushed one more time, charged with all the power of her hopelessness, the bolt finally gave way. After half an hour of relentless labour, the door was open. She found herself in the middle of the street, and it didn't even cross her mind to shut the door behind her.

The night had permeated everything with its stillness and darkness. There was not a star or a candlelight to be seen, nor a sound to be heard in the infinity of the night. Only the distant barking of dogs and the awful echoes of piercing wind gusts blowing inside the Byzantine ruins reached her fearful ears. She walked across the neighbourhood with her head down, taking hasty steps, until she came across the ruins of a burned-down place. She suddenly stopped in front of a house. The terrifying silence of the night and the ghastly sounds coming from the ruins haunted the tiny heart of this creature who longed for kindness, affection and protection. A penetrating wind from the ice-capped mountains of the north crept into her body, setting every nerve shivering. Memories of Taravet's cruelty and her mistress's oppression flooded back into her frail heart and mind, already paralysed by the brutal cold and horror. As the terror of her vivid imagination reigned over her like a tyrant, she finally collapsed to her knees.

And then, as her weary eyes absorbed the scene as though in a dream, just over there, at the far edge of the horizon, under a sky veiled by black velvet, appeared an illusion, a misty light. Looking more closely at this sudden, heavenly glow, she saw within it the smiling face of her mother. There she was, smiling at her! Dilber thought she could almost hear her voice. Ah, her mother was coming towards her. The child stretched her withered arms, weakened by hard work, towards the sky to embrace her dear mother. 'Please help me!' she said. Then she fell onto her back with a bitter cry and fainted.

Chapter 2

When she woke up from a deep sleep, Dilber found herself in an unfamiliar bed in an unfamiliar house. Before her stood an elderly woman, an old face wrinkled with the traces of time. She was watching over Dilber with a gentle and affectionate gaze as the subtle spark of her soul glimmered through the clouds in her eyes. With shaky hands, she was giving Dilber medicine, and yet it was undoubtedly her compassionate eyes that offered the real remedy for the little one's aching heart. Her long grey hair, which must have enchanted so many in her youth, fell over Dilber's face, creating quite a scene. What better shelter could there be for that tormented soul than this heavenly, luminous spread?

The room in which they had put her was a modest one. There was one large and one small floor cushion. Aside from a few small mats scattered about and an old, recessed niche displaying a Çanakkale-style earthenware jug and cup, the room was sparsely furnished. Dilber was awake, sitting up in bed, holding the doll that they had placed beside her. When the old woman noticed that the child was awake, she gently asked:

'My dear child, whose daughter are you?'

'I am a slave', replied Dilber.

After a moment of reflection, the old woman stroked Dilber's hair with her soft and trembling hands:

'Whose slave girl are you?' she asked.

'My mistress's'.

'Who's your mistress?'

'Miss Atiye's mother'.

The old woman paused for another moment. Then she asked again:

'Why were you out on the street late last night, my girl?'

Dilber didn't respond.

Chapter 2

'How did you come all the way here, my child?' The old woman asked. 'Weren't you scared of the shadows of the night or of the ghoul that appears to naughty children?'

Once again, Dilber remained silent.

'You were calling your dear mother in your sleep last night. Who's your mother? Where is she now? Tell me, my child'.

'I don't know', said Dilber.

The old woman wiped away her tears. 'I'll send my granddaughter in so you two can play together', she said and left the room. A few minutes later, a girl came in through the door. After a quick glance, the girl ran towards Dilber's bed, and the two were instantly locked in an embrace. Only then did Dilber realise that this was her classmate Lütfiye.

'What happened to you, Dilber?' Lütfiye asked.

'Nothing. I escaped', Dilber replied.

'Why did you escape?'

'They beat me a lot; they make me work all the time, and every minute of every hour they call me a filthy Circassian or a filthy slave. I am not allowed to play any games, and if I ever sit by the hearth to warm up, Taravet scorches my hands with the fire iron. Here, look at my arm', she said. She pulled her arm from underneath the bed cover. There really was a burn scar on her dark and hardened skin. Dilber continued talking:

'Maybe you can carry this mattress downstairs, and I can be your slave. Please let me be your slave. I'll carry water for you. I'll dress up your dolls. I'll sweep your room. Please don't make me leave!'

'I can hide you here in the closet', Lütfiye said. 'No one can find you or take you away'.

How heartbreaking it was to hear a child's plea for help from another child! How moving it was to witness a child's naive and protective promise: 'I'll hide you here in the closet', coming straight from a loving, friendly heart. As the young girls settled on their secret escape plan, their heavenly, innocent faces brightened with joy. Poor children! Your tiny little hands were not meant to break the chains of slavery – a burden of ancient Asian civilisations – that crushed humanity under its oppressive weight for centuries. Your hands were meant to stroke the feathers of little birds and to caress the petals of flowers, as delicate as you yourselves.

After talking to Dilber, Lütfiye ran to her grandmother and despairingly explained to her, as best she could, whose slave Dilber was and how much agony and suffering she had endured. The old woman walked over to Dilber.

'Don't fear, my beautiful child', she said calmly, guided by her faith and a clear conscience, and comforted the child with gentle affection. Here was a life nearing its end, offering solace to a life just beginning. The old woman took a scarf to cover her head and grabbed her cane to steady her frail body, then left the house. In the deepest corner of her ninety-year-old heart, somewhere amongst the unfulfilled wishes and lost hopes, a desire stirred to save this little girl. Just like a lantern would guide one through darkness, this very desire now guided her through her sorrow. She wished to save this child as an act of worship and devotion to God. She headed straight to Mustafa Efendi's house and knocked on the door.

That very morning, Taravet noticed that Dilber wasn't in her bed. First, she checked the yard, thinking the girl may be out carrying water, but Dilber wasn't there either. Later, she searched the entire house, again to no avail. When she finally went downstairs and noticed that the gate was wide open, she started to get suspicious. Suddenly questions flooded her mind: Had Dilber run away? Where had she spent the night? Had stray dogs torn her to pieces? Unable to comprehend how Dilber could have managed to make an escape plan, let alone dare to commit the crime of causing her mistress material loss, Taravet hastened to her mistress's room in panic and started yelling:

'Ah, my mistress, Dilber has escaped, Dilber has escaped!'

The mistress was stupefied by the news.

'What do you mean, Dilber has escaped? Have you gone mad? What would a child of that age know about escaping?' she asked. Taravet had no idea where Dilber was, but you could read the fury on her face. Her eyes widened, their whites stark, like dim candles against the dark backdrop of her face. Her voice trembled. Her mouth was agape, revealing shiny white teeth that resembled the ivory keys through the lid of a black piano. Overwhelmed by panic and unable to think, she tried to explain the situation to her mistress: 'If she didn't escape... wouldn't she be in the yard? Her closet... Her clothes... The door is wide open... She's not here... She is not anywhere'.

The mistress lost her temper. 'It's all your fault', she yelled at Taravet. 'Now, go and find her, immediately. Or else I'll beat you until your last breath!' Taravet covered her head and went out on the street, asking everyone whom she encountered whether they had stolen her mistress's slave girl.

In the meantime, the old woman arrived in Mustafa Efendi's house. When she entered the room, the mistress stood up and started talking anxiously:

'Ah, auntie! You have no idea what happened. That cursed slave girl of mine, that filthy Circassian, has run away'.

'No, my girl', the old woman said in a calm and soft voice. 'Your slave girl did not run away. She is at my house'.

When the mistress heard this, she froze in astonishment, like a statue. The old woman continued talking.

'My girl, just as God forgives the sins of children, mistresses should excuse their mistakes. I came here to plead with you. Allow me to give you the five pouches of silver coins that I have saved, and you give me the girl in return', she suggested.

'What are you going to do with her?' the mistress asked. The old woman attempted a light-hearted reply, trying to resolve the situation in her favour.

'I will free a bird on Holy Night', she said with a twinkle in her eyes.

'I am not selling my slave to anyone', said the mistress in her usual unpleasant way. Taken aback by this rejection, the old woman replied:

'And I am not returning a child who ran away from oppression and sought refuge with me'.

'Is your house a den of thieves?' Mustafa Efendi cut in. The old woman remained silent. 'Isn't she my slave?' the wretched, disrespectful brute yelled. 'I'd rather kill her than sell her to you!'

Hearing these words, the old woman rose. She fixed her piercing eyes, which had already stared into the dizzying abyss of life, on Mustafa Efendi's ugly face. With his long and round nose above a small black hole of a mouth, bushy eyebrows and slanted eyes, he looked like a raptor. His thick, pitch-black beard and moustache, typical of people from around Iran, added to his repulsive demeanour. The old woman held her gaze on Mustafa Efendi for a moment, then shook her head in contempt. With the authority of a majestic Roman emperor, she declared: 'Damn you both!' She then quickly covered her head and left the house.

On the way back, the old woman groaned with every step she took until she reached her home. Dilber was there. She walked up to the child and kissed her on the eyes with her sunken, divine lips – lips that prayed to God all day long.

'Don't worry, my child', she said. 'God who gives butterflies wings to fly would not leave you in their hands forever. Now, go back to your mistress. Don't be afraid, my dear child. From now on they won't beat you'. At that moment, there was a knock on the door, and the old woman stuck her head out the oriel window to see who it was. When she saw that it was the imam, she asked: 'What do you want, Imam Efendi?' Imam Efendi responded: 'I came to get Mustafa Efendi's slave girl. She should come down right away!'

The old woman and Dilber looked at each other. Tears weighed down the dim, aging eyes of the compassionate host, while Dilber's eyes silently cried for help. Imam Efendi was summoning Dilber back to her dungeon of torment. She looked at her with pleading eyes. His voice had terrified her in the way in which the rumbling of thunder terrifies children's hearts.

No doubt these two wounded souls could feel each other's innocence and agonising pain. The old woman kept wiping away her tears while she held the child in her arms. When it was time to part, the old woman carried Dilber out of the room in her arms. Dilber played with the henna-dyed ends of the old woman's grey hair, the last beams of sunset of a ninety-five-year-old life that fell on her face. But she wasn't crying at all. If crying shows the body's last remnant of strength in its struggle against the misfortunes that befall us, then the moments when we cannot cry are those in which even that final strength has failed us. In those moments, our cries are replaced by an intense silence that is more heart-rending than sad sobs. It was in such a state of silence that Dilber came downstairs, holding the imam's hand right away, and started walking.

Poor child! This was the second time that she realised in her short life, now with harder evidence than ever before, how helpless she was in the claws of captivity, stronger than iron, colder than death. When she returned to the prison of torment, she realised that she was once again being handed over by a ruinous power to suffering, dismay and hard labour; all that she hopelessly tried to escape with the strength and courage left in her body and soul. Her innocent soul and childish mind were utterly helpless against an immense power that defied all explanations and reason, yet this power held her captive. Dilber was shaking from head to toe as she stepped through the door.

Suddenly, she heard her mistress yelling from the top of the stairs: 'Keep that wicked girl out of my sight. Lock her up in the closet!' Dilber kept quiet. Taravet kicked her from behind towards the inside of the cabinet. Dilber fell on her face, and a few drops of blood trickled down. Yet she did not shed a single tear. Taravet locked her up in the closet before she left. Dilber could hear the mice walking around. Of all the animals she feared, she feared mice the most, even more so than snakes. And yet not once did she flinch inside the cabinet.

It was now three in the morning.[1] The closet was still locked. Dilber had only had a little bit of cheese and bread to eat since the morning.

[1] In the nineteenth century, the Ottomans used sundials to calculate the exact position of the sun as well as time. The day was divided into two sets of twelve units as day and night. Daytime started with sunrise, and nighttime started with sunset. Hence, three in the morning would be three hours after sunrise. For more information on *alaturka* hours, see Wishnitzer's *Reading Clocks Alla Turca*.

Like all young people, she had an insatiable appetite; she couldn't help it. She was hungry, and hunger manifested itself in violent stomach cramps. When they finally let her out of her confinement, she was given a piece of bread to eat. She ate her bread, went to her room and made her bed in utter silence; then she changed her clothes and went to bed. Fearing that Taravet would hear her and beat her or, even worse, tell the mistress about it, Dilber pulled the cover over her head, put her tiny hands over her aching face and sobbed violently, crying: 'Mommy, mommy!'

Chapter 3

It was all quiet. Dilber was sleeping. Her tiny little face was resting on the pillow moistened by her tears, her tousled hair covering her face, her mouth slightly open, her lips curved into an almost smile. It was as if she were waiting for her mother to kiss her on the lips, or, if her mother was resting in the silence of her grave, for an angel sent by her mother in heaven to deliver to her little girl the soft, motherly kiss that soothed a child's pain.

Alas! This frail creature who had been crushed by captivity, forsaken by humanity and only occasionally caressed by hope was now being lulled into oblivion in the arms of the night. As the first rays of dawn, as pale as her complexion, tried to find their way through her window, she rubbed her eyes with her hands.

But that day, something miraculous happened – like a divine intervention that arrives unexpectedly to rescue our broken hearts in our final moments, when our woes peak. Something was impending to transform Dilber's life, which, until now, like a river carving its way through steeped mountains and dark forests, had flowed through endless hardships and agony. It so happened that on the same day that Mustafa Efendi was cleared on all counts of bribery, he was assigned to a town in the city of Erzurum as district governor. But that wasn't all. While he was under investigation, Mustafa Efendi had run up an enormous debt, and now he was looking for a way to pay off his debts so that he would have the means to move his family to the province of Erzurum. After a couple of days of going back and forth, he and his wife decided to sell Dilber to cover the cost of their move to Erzurum.

Poor Dilber! Just as she had endured all kinds of torment when Mustafa Efendi had been out of work – carrying the weight of the entire house on her tiny shoulders – she was once again put to work, this time to pay for Mustafa Efendi's debts and travel expenses with her frail body. Overjoyed at the thought of her husband's turn of luck, Mustafa Efendi's wife now tamed her customary temper toward Dilber and said things such as: 'Would I ever sell you if I thought you could change, but you are hopeless. God help your next mistress!'

One of those days, Mustafa Efendi received orders to report to his post in Erzurum immediately. Thus, they had to act right away. Within a week, they had found a slave trader and sold Dilber for sixty liras. Then they left Istanbul for Trabzon on a Wednesday, on the Lloyd Company's steamboat.[1]

[1] The Austrian shipping company Lloyd was founded in 1833 and offered scheduled voyages between Istanbul and various cities around the Black Sea and the Mediterranean starting in 1844.

Chapter 4

Figure 9 Edirnekapı city walls. Courtesy of IBB Atatürk Library.

Somewhere around the Edirnekapı neighbourhood, there stood a big, impressive, yet dreary house built in the Ottoman architectural style of the early 1800s. The ravages of time, which have buried even the most thriving cities and greatest civilisations, were now pulling this house down at its corners. The right side of the house bore traces of the architectural style of the previous millennium. Inside, a capacious room held a long floor cushion, its cotton stuffing bulging from the frayed corners, alongside a few extra pillows in rotting, threadbare covers. The windows offered views of vast ruins, reduced to ashes by a great, destructive fire at an unknown time, yet long attributed to Janissary cruelty and assaults. Then there were the overhanging eaves, stretched out like two big black wings, preventing the sunlight from entering the house. One could feel the suffocating humidity in the hall and see the plaster peeling off the damp walls. From this hall, one could see a big vegetable garden, and at its far end stood one of the most barbaric places of the Middle Ages: a terrifying dungeon.[1] The house stood by itself in this forsaken place, surrounded by big vegetable gardens. Wild birds, such as owls and hawks, nested inside the eaves of its façade that overlooked the Byzantine ruins. Their heart-wrenching cries filled the air at dusk, deepening the gloom hanging over the dreary house.[2] The sky was veiled, and the house only revealed its melancholic face through the clouds brought in by the south-westerly winds. It was as if it were inhabited by ghosts that escaped from the yonder dungeon at midnight.

The woeful moonlight trickling through the ancient skylights cast a faded silhouette of Dilber as she went up the stairs, carrying a tray. The part of the house overlooking the vegetable gardens was rented by a slave trader. The people who lived there often whispered tales of ghosts that emerged from the dilapidated, long-abandoned quarter and wandered through the halls and dark corners of the house at night. In fact, one of the slaves claimed to have seen a ghost staring right into her eyes, as if it had something to say to her. This eerie house with all its mysteries weighed heavy on Dilber's heart, bringing on an inexplicable feeling of sorrow and anguish. And naturally, like all children, she was frightened by this feeling and needed a tremendous amount of strength and courage to deliver food to the ailing slave trader's room late at night. But where to muster all that strength and courage when her strength and courage had already been crushed by her wrathful, cruel old mistress and Taravet?

Carrying the plate from the kitchen to the slave trader's room thus meant taxing herself to her very limits, a task that brought great agony upon her soul. Dilber walked up the stairs with the food tray in her hands. As she passed by a hall bathed in melancholic moonlight, an owl hooted from the other side. Dilber froze in fear as an owl's cry pierced through the thick silence of the night, cutting through the dilapidated walls of the

[1] The Prison of Anemas, a significant Byzantine structure attached to the Walls of Constantinople in the Edirnekapı district, was named after Michael Anemas, a Byzantine general who conspired against Emperor Alexios I Komnenos (r. 1081–1118). Anemas was the initial prisoner tortured there. See Figure 10.

[2] The Palace of the Porphyrogenitus (Tekfur Sarayı) is a thirteenth-century Byzantine palace built as an extension to the Palace of the Blachernae on the northern corner of the Theodosian Walls, between the Edirnekapı and Eğrikapı neighbourhoods. Due to its proximity to the outer walls, the palace sustained severe damage during the Ottoman conquest of Constantinople in 1453. See Figure 11.

Figure 10 The Prison of Anemas. Courtesy of IBB Atatürk Library.

Figure 11 The Palace of the Porphyrogenitus. Courtesy of IBB Atatürk Library.

ruins. She hesitated for a moment and then quickly hurried into the slave trader woman's room. Seeing Dilber's face, the slave trader said: 'What happened, child? Your face has turned ashen'.

'My mistress, there's a dreadful bird crying out there, well…'

'You foolish girl! How could you be so scared of a bird? Stop worrying and fussing so much; it's making you look ugly. Just go out, have fun and try to appear charming. Hopefully, buyers will fancy you, and you will be sold to a good home. Your life will be better, and I'll make some money. Now go and play your oud'.[3]

After this brief conversation, Dilber left the slave trader's bedroom and walked across the hall, to a much more pleasant room where there was a long white floor cushion in front of the windows and an oil lamp burning on the small table. A few stools and pillows were scattered around the room. Mattresses were stacked in an alcove, and around the alcove musical instruments such as ouds and violins were hanging on the wall. All the slave girls in that house had gathered in this room. One was sitting on the big cushion all by herself, her legs crossed, her untied hair naturally falling on her knees, as she played the oud. Another was seated on the long cushion, sewing. One was lost in a book, while two other slave girls were talking to each other.

They conversed enthusiastically about the Caucasus, remembering its towering mountains whose peaks almost grazed the blue skies, its enchanting wild forests where morning birds were singing all kinds of songs, its colourful rivers mirroring nearby flowers, meadows and clouds, as they flowed gracefully from the peaks. They reminisced about its crystal-clear waters cascading in rhythm, nourishing the soul, and the joy of dancing to the tunes that they played on their traditional instruments along the riverbanks.[4]

The slave girl who had previously been engrossed in her reading closed her book and, with a contemplative melancholy etched across her innocent face, directed her gaze towards the light: 'How hard it is to serve them from a young age on and suffer through their whims and caprices…', she said. 'And then one day, just because you refuse to surrender yourself to the advances of the master's ugly, despicable son, they send you back to the slave trader's house, just like that, with lies and slander, without even a probe into what really happened'. She then stood up from her floor cushion and walked towards the other two slave girls who were talking to each other.

[3] Musical entertainment played a crucial role in the harems of the Ottoman court and private households alike. Consequently, many female slaves were instructed in the art of playing musical instruments, with the oud (short-necked lute) being particularly popular.

[4] Sezai's depiction of the Caucasus presented in this context aligns with the romanticised portrayal of the region commonly found first in Russian Romantic literature and then in European travel writings of the nineteenth century. See Susan Layton, *Russian Literature and Empire: Conquest of the Caucasus from Pushkin to Tolstoy* and Charles King, *The Ghost of Freedom: A History of the Caucasus.*

'Ah, Şayeste', she said to one of the slave girls. 'Those happy days, the cheerful dreams, the sweet memories… As I watch them pass before my eyes these past few days, my restless heart longs to follow in their wake. Oh, how I miss everything, even the trees in my childhood home. Only now do I realize that the rose bush in our garden was more than a rose bush; it was my friend. All the rooms, every single corner in that house, all the faces around me were a part of my childhood, part of a happy time in my life. And now, look at me. I am being sold to a stranger, to an unfamiliar household'. The slave girl began weeping as she uttered these last words.

When she saw the slave girl cry, Dilber immediately went to the door to make sure the slave trader was not around. She knew that, if the slave trader were to find the girls gathered in a room, sharing their secrets and, even worse, crying, it was certain that they all would be punished.

Dilber looked back at the slave girl from the threshold. She was still crying. Dilber could tell that she was thinking about her beloved. In front of her tearful, light-blue eyes lingered the memory of him. He was right there, his image as vivid as Venus set aflame on a misty night. But she kept quiet. Clearly, it was a memory of which she never wished to speak.

And the other slave girl, the one sewing in the corner... She had once been a gentle house cat, now transformed into a ferocious tiger by her master's relentless whippings; a lamb that had become a wolf through violence and insults. One day, overwhelmed by despair, this frail slave girl, who had endured countless beatings, assault and humiliation, had turned into a tigress and unexpectedly rebelled against her masters. She had torn everything she could get her hands on, had crushed her mistress's traditional bib necklace – embroidered with the most precious jewels – under her foot and had committed an even more horrifying offense… an unspeakable offense… she had set her master's house on fire.

This time all the slave girls gathered around the oil lamp to listen to the girl with the oud to tell her story. She recounted how she had fallen in love with a young, handsome pasha, how he at first had returned her love, but when her mistress discovered this little romance between her husband and the slave girl, how she was immediately sold off. 'How heart-rending and humiliating it is now to cry over my love for the pasha in a slave trader's house', she said in a shaky voice. Embarrassed by what she was about to say, she lowered her gaze. 'But, in the end, she should not have punished me because of her husband's wrong-doing', she said, trying to be fair to her mistress but also to herself. Love, loss, affection, oppression, the agony of captivity, the sharing of secrets…

Chapter 4

Right in the middle of their conversation, the door suddenly slammed open! Dilber had failed in her duty of guarding the door. The slave trader had strictly prohibited any kind of intimate conversation among the slave girls, especially the sharing of secrets, knowing that it would constitute a threat to her trade. But clearly the slave girls had gone against her orders. She had overheard their most intimate conversations through the door and burst into the room in a fit of rage, with a whip in her hand. What a heartbreaking scene this was… What a tragic spectacle it was to witness…

As the whip started to execute its orders with force and fury, the slave girls began to scream and scatter in every direction. But the whip followed them and lashed their naked bodies. Yes, these girls had once been slaves in the houses of the most prominent families, nurtured with their love and care. But these masters had not hesitated to sell these girls off for trivial, capricious reasons and petty excuses. And yet, even these brutal, heartless masters would be touched by this scene.

A few minutes after the slave trader had forced the slave girls to repent under the force of her whip, silence enveloped the room, and she separated them from each other. Dilber, meanwhile, was placed in one of the rooms overlooking the gardens. Although deeply moved by the stories of the slave girls, she had not spoken or shared anything herself, and for this reason she had been spared from the slave trader's punishment.

'Sleep here and keep quiet', the slave trader ordered her and waited in the room until Dilber had made her bed and lit the oil lamp. She then shut the door and started to walk down the hall. Dilber listened as the footsteps gradually vanished into the night, and when she could no longer hear them, only then did she realise that she was all alone in this big, cold, tomb-like room.

As soon as she crawled into the bed, shivers ran through her entire body. Only a couple of minutes later did she manage to lift her tiny head, heavy with memories of her life's painful moments, from the pillow. She listened. No… Not a creak… No… Not a whisper. Absolutely nothing. She wrapped the bed cover tightly around her shivering body and sat up straight in her bed. Suddenly, a rather heart-wrenching, ugly sound, like a shriek almost, came from behind her, from where the fallen towers and walls of those thousand-year-old Byzantine ruins stood. She tried to get up from her bed like a wounded bird, fluttering its wings.

Oh, it was the owl hooting. Oh! This sound! This ominous, terrible sound! That old superstition, passed on from generation to generation for centuries – that an owl hoot was bad luck, an ill omen – had now found itself a tiny hiding place in this young girl's mind. The weak oil lamp ebbed and flowed, lighting only one side of the room and leaving the rest in the dark. Dilber kept staring at the wall. The shadow play of the thin black smoke rising from the oil lamp created ever bigger shapes as her eyes stayed in their fixed spot. To her fearful eyes, these shapes looked like terrifying figures dressed in white, wearing black caps, like the image of Taravet, walking up to her with a piece of hot, charred firewood. Finally, she placed her head on the pillow and pulled the bed cover over her head.

The owl kept hooting.

Ever since the day she had arrived at the house, people had been talking about the presence of ghosts. Now, in this pitch-black night, she could hear their footsteps coming closer from the direction of the dungeon, that lonely structure covered in thick fog, revealing only its majestic dome. All her hair stood on end.

The owl kept hooting.

All Dilber could think of was to get out of the room and run as fast as she could to the slave trader's room and sleep there. But it was too late. The doorway had already been invaded by ghosts. She thought of jumping from the window. It's not very high, she thought, looking at the window.

The owl kept hooting.

Dilber pulled the bed cover tightly over her head and covered her ears with her hands. But it was in vain. The laughter and chatter of the night ghosts still drifted through the windows and doors. She lifted her head from the pillow, listening in fear. This time, there was only silence.

The sun was coming up! The morning sun left its seat in the East and streamed through the window above Dilber's head in the shape of two pillars of light. Dilber imagined them as if they were her mother's arms reaching out to her from Heaven, to protect and rescue her. Her restless heart nestled in her arms, and she finally drifted into a deep sleep.

Chapter 5

It was four o'clock in the morning. The slave trader went downstairs and started knocking on Dilber's door. It was locked from inside, and nobody responded. She kept knocking, calling out her name: 'Dilber, Dilber!' Still, there was no answer. After staying awake for so long and fighting the fears and trepidations that haunted her, Dilber had finally fallen into a deep sleep. The slave trader knocked on the door for a third time, now more forcefully, still calling Dilber's name at the top of her voice. But still there was no response from Dilber. Anxiously, the slave trader climbed on a stool, reached through the gap in the door to grasp the upper latch, then stepped down and repeated the process with the lower one. At last, she pushed the door open. By then, all that noise had woken Dilber.

'Dilber, what happened to you? How come you overslept?' the slave trader asked.

'I was so scared last night. This room... It was horrible', Dilber replied, with tears in her eyes.

The slave trader was now thinking about her profits and the damage that her business would suffer should Dilber's health be scarred by fear. 'Ah, my girl! What's there to fear?' she said, trying to reassure her. 'Would I have ever left you alone in this room if I knew you were so easily scared? From now on, sleep with me in the same bed, every night'. Then she kissed the girl on the eyes, patted her on the shoulder. 'Come on, get up, my girl. You have good customers interested in buying you. Wash your face and change', she said and then left the room.

Obeying the slave trader's orders, Dilber went upstairs to greet the new buyers. She kissed the hem of the new mistress's dress. The slave trader then praised Dilber's talent for playing the oud and her ability to read and write. She explained to the mistress that the girl's pallor was due to a recent cold and blamed her frailty on the relentless effort she devoted to her studies. Shortly thereafter, the slave trader sold Dilber for 150 liras, with the assurance that, if any fault were to be found with her, she could be returned within a week. The slave trader added that, if the girl hadn't been so ugly, she would have demanded 200 liras.

It was true what the slave trader had told the customers: Dilber looked pale and frail. The tragedies and hardships that she had endured during adolescence had cast a dark shadow over her young face. Hardship and suffering had etched tiny wrinkles across her skin, like withered rose petals that bloomed before their time, and her cheeks had visibly sagged. This twelve-year-old body now bore the face of a fifty-year-old woman.

A week later, the slave trader handed over the bond stating that she accepted silver coins in exchange for Dilber.

Chapter 6

'How tiny! Praise be to these black eyes. The face, the mouth, the lips… beautiful. Just beautiful. This pale colour, this melancholic gaze will inspire an ever-sorrowful painting… What now, are you feeling ill?'

'No'.

'Then why do you look so pale?'

'I don't know'.

'Your age?'

'Fifteen'.

'Are you from the Caucasus? Or are you from İzmit?'

'…'

'Take a look at the dark green trees, the forests over there; look at the blue skies with your black eyes. Did you come from a land of such colours?'

'Yes'.

'Your name?'

'Dilber'.

Night unveiled itself over the dark-blue, crystalline waters of the Sea of Marmara, where at sunset the sun's rays withdrew and the world's babble fell silent, where at midnight the fairies bathed. It draped the sea in a blue satin sheet embroidered with pearls, woven from the luminous traces that the stars cast down from the glass-coloured sky, like lovers' glances.

Celal Bey was sitting in his armchair on the balcony of a mansion by the sea, smoking his cigarette and watching the Bosphorus. Somewhere in the distance, a cluster of stars cast their shimmering reflection on the water. It looked as if faint moonlight danced across its surface. Further away, tiny waves brushed the horizon amorously, like a lover kissing his beloved on the lips with a fluttering heart, before they disappeared into the blue shadows in haste.

Celal Bey reflected calmly on the last five years he had spent studying art in Paris, on the vibrant memories of his life of twenty-three years, still untouched by sorrow, and on a beautiful smile or a sweet glance that he had caught in the hidden corners of his Parisian circles. He watched these recollections ripple across the sea, that silent mirror of secrets.

Thanks to his natural talent in painting and impeccable education, Celal Bey had earned a prestigious opportunity to present one of his paintings at the Salon.[1] It was the painting of a three-oared rowing boat, gliding through the melancholic waters of the Bosphorus. It depicted two women whose rose-coloured cheeks and sparkling black eyes could only be seen through a thin veil. Behind them on the rowing boat was an imperial African eunuch; everyone was seated on a shawl decorated with tassels dangling down the sides.[2]

The selection committee at the Salon had commended this talented apprentice of Gérôme yet offered one critique: they had found the blue colour of the Bosphorus, the abundance and brightness of the light that fell from the sky like wheat sheaves to be overly exaggerated in the painting.[3] Celal had responded to the committee with a letter defending his painting, arguing: 'Upon careful observation, one would see that exaggerating any colour is impossible on a sunny day in the Orient, where the luminous sky reveals even the celestial figures soaring far beyond human comprehension'. And with that letter, he had achieved the honour of having his remarkable work of art accepted by the Salon.

With his rather sizable body, his hazel eyes, his vibrant and colourful disposition – all signs of his hot bodily humours – Celal looked like a Roman. Because he had always been blessed with perfect health and was

[1] The Paris Salon served as the official art exhibition of the Académie des Beaux-Arts in Paris.

[2] Celal Bey's painting, as described in this context, resembles one of the drawings by Jean Brindesi, a local artist who was born and died in Istanbul. This drawing, commonly titled *Bateau (Kaiq)* and dating to 1845, was part of his collection *Souvenirs de Constantinople*, which was lithographed by Lemercier in Paris in 1860. See Figure 12.

[3] Jean-Léon Gérôme (1824–1904), a French painter and sculptor known for his Orientalist scenes from the Middle East and North Africa, also served as professor of painting at the École des Beaux-Arts. He is mostly known for his 1879 oil paintings *The Snake Charmer* and *Veiled Circassian Woman* (1876). He was widely known among the Ottoman elite and visited Istanbul in 1875. See Mary Roberts' *Istanbul Exchanges*. During the 1860s, the period in which *The Adventures of a Slave Girl* is set, Gérôme had Ottoman students, akin to Celal Bey depicted in the novel, who were studying art under his tutelage. Among these students, Osman Hamdi Bey (1842–1910) stands out as the most renowned, becoming Turkey's first Orientalist painter and the founder of both the Istanbul Archaeology Museum and the Istanbul Academy of Fine Arts.

Figure 12 Jean Brindesi, *Bateau* (*Kaiq*). Sezai's inspiration for Celal's painting *Souvenirs de Constantinople*, Paris, Imp. Lemercier, 1845. Courtesy of the Gennadius Library.

treated kindly by life itself, he had a joyful and light-hearted disposition. Celal was in the spring of his life. And yet, although he was in the brightest and most passioned time of youth, which, like spring, awakens flowers to bloom in the lands through which it passes and stirs affection in hearts, he felt within himself no inclination, no appetite for love or attachment,and would proudly confess now and then, with concealed hopelessness, that the only love in his heart was the love for his high art. Only in rare moments would his heart whisper to him, as one of its most hidden feelings, that he had fallen under the spell of a sultana of beauty who, like a divine torch, had crossed the dense darkness of past centuries and now sat enthroned in the sacred temple of ancient Greece, crowned with spring flowers from the eastern lands.

Celal's father was a wealthy man. He had previously held various government positions in Egypt and, during that time, had amassed a fortune for himself. Upon his return to Istanbul, he had poured money into building a European-style mansion on the shores of the Moda neighbourhood.[4]

[4] A coastal neighbourhood in the Kadıköy district of Istanbul, located on the Anatolian side. In the late nineteenth century, Moda became highly popular among Ottoman non-Muslims and Europeans, who built large mansions there.

This was a spectacular mansion. Its façade faced the sea, while the landward side was surrounded by imposing sycamore, chestnut and olive trees that offered glimpses of the dark-blue sky to wandering eye. The sunshine danced as the trees swayed elegantly in the sky and imbued the secluded garden with the tranquillity and peace for which any soul yearns.

The lower floor of the mansion facing the garden featured a grand drawing room with a large marble fireplace whose mantel was adorned with jambs shaped in the form of two naked mermaids from mythological tales. A large mirror hung above the fireplace, and a white bearskin was spread on the floor beneath it. At the centre of the room stood a Louis-XIV table, an elegant work of art, encircled by chairs with gilded legs and backrests. There was also a small, exquisitely crafted writing desk from the same period. The sofas, designed like attached armchairs, were arranged to face each other, creating an intimate setting for quiet conversation and private exchanges.[5] Behind the sofas, in the corners of the room, stood planters, crafted to resemble ancient metalwork, filled with lush plants from Africa and India, with their flowers nearly reaching the ceiling. The floor was covered with kilims, exquisite examples of Anatolian carpet-weaving, layered with the pelts of rare animals. Two paintings adorned the dark-red wallpaper, patterned with gold accents. The first of these was a magnificent painting depicting the triumphant entry of Mehmed the Conqueror into Istanbul, full of grandeur and majesty.[6] The other one, hanging on the opposite side, regally depicted Napoleon I on the rocky cliffs of Saint Helena, engulfed in fog, his gaze directed at the horizon, towards Europe, conquering the scene with the eyes of a magnificent eagle.[7]

In the right corner of the fireplace of this richly decorated drawing room was a grand piano. In the evenings, Asaf Pasha's nineteen-year-old daughter, ready to unlock the gilded gates of the palace of secret love, would play a romantic piece on the piano, her fingers spreading joy, awakening hidden feelings and gently caressing the soul.

[5] The sofas described here are two- or three-seater couches imported from Europe, replacing the divans in Europeanised houses.

[6] This seems to be a direct reference to the French Orientalist painter Jean-Joseph Benjamin-Constant's 1876 painting titled *The Entry of Sultan Mehmet II into Constantinople*. See Figure 13.

[7] Even though there exist various paintings depicting Napoleon's time on St Helena, based on the description above we firmly believe that Sezai is referencing the British painter Benjamin Robert Haydon (1786–1846)'s famous *Napoleon Bonaparte Musing at St Helena*. Haydon's Bonaparte musing on his fortunes and misfortunes was so popular that the painting exists in over twenty replicas. See Figure 14.

Figure 13 Benjamin Constant, *The Entry of Mehmet II into Constantinople* (1876). Courtesy of Musée des Augustins, Ville de Toulouse.

After dinner, the members of the household would gather here, when the room was bathed in a soft blue glow from the colourful shades of the oil lamps, and read newspapers and books. Some nights, Asaf Pasha, the head of the household, would play cards with his wife, while Celal Bey would enjoy his sister's piano-playing and flip

Figure 14 Benjamin Robert Haydon, *Napoléon on St Helena* (1846). Courtesy of National Portrait Gallery in London.

through the pages of the illustrated newspapers alongside his French governess.

The small door near the windows led to the winter garden, which then opened to the afore-mentioned garden. On the same floor as the grand salon was also a dining room with blue satin curtains hanging from its high windows. Through the gaps in the curtains, one's gaze wandered among the flowers in the garden, paused by the edge of the pond, drifted off into the treetops in a daydream and fell into the green darkness of the forest, weary and tired.

The elderly French lady with whom Celal Bey often perused illustrated newspapers was his sister Tesliye's governess. Despite having lived in Istanbul for over a decade, she had learned only a few Turkish phrases such as 'Let's see... Kismet... Slowly slowly...' However, when it came to her own national language, French, she wanted to teach it to everyone with the same fervour with which missionaries spread Protestantism. She even used to say: 'Humanity must learn the language of Voltaire, Hugo and Jean Jacques Rousseau'. How astonished she was when she heard that the Turkish language had its own distinct literature, not entirely convinced that this could be the case. In her early days in Istanbul, during a dinner conversation about languages, she had suggested that 'Turkish must have been derived from the language spoken by the Byzantines'. When people laughed at her remarks, she went on to speculate further: 'Or could it be from the Arabic spoken in Egypt today?' Realising that this was not the case either, she became frustrated and exclaimed: 'It's impossible to know; in the East, the truth is veiled like the women!'

Whenever the subject of London came up in a conversation, the governess would say that she never quite understood why people would ever live in a dark city buried under the fog year-round when there was the bright and sunny Paris nearby. She would always tell the story of a cold Sunday in London, back when she had spent a winter there as governess: 'Not a soul passes by on the streets where low-hanging clouds almost touch the roofs. Nothing is open, except for the churches. If you ever wonder how a city of four million people suddenly looks like a dead town, as if suddenly struck by a tragedy, visit London on a Sunday in December'. She would then add: 'Isn't it curious how people pass by, cutting through the dark mist like a spectre; go into those huge parks and listen to sermons about death under the perpetual rain; without catching the quintessential English malady, melancholia, as they walk from one end of the street to the other?' trying to show off her eloquence and wit as she talked, in that typical French manner. On days when she put on her glasses and read a French newspaper, she would say in an arrogant manner, like old diplomats addressing the parliament: 'It won't take long now, it is certain that there will be a war against the Germans next spring'. Or, whenever someone said, 'Have you heard the news today?', she would respond: 'What is it? Did France declare war against Germany?' It so happened that the owners of the house had requested this very governess to serve as Dilber's French tutor as well.

Dilber was happy in this house. Each morning, she would tidy the rooms of the mistress and her daughter and then take care of the canary, cleaning its cage, feeding it and replenishing its water. From time to time, she would watch the canary flap its wings fiercely inside the cage and laugh with the innocent glee of a child. Then she would talk to it, saying:

'Look at you, all dressed up in yellow, my little slave girl. Behave and be good in your little palace, will you? If you make any mischief, I'll send you off to Taravet'.

Perhaps one could say that her life in this household was comfortable, but the fear that had once gripped her heart when it was still young and tender would not leave her now, settling there like an obsessive thought. And so, whenever one of her masters called out 'Dilber!' she would rush upstairs, trembling in fear. She believed that, whatever task she had completed, she must have done something wrong that deserved a beating or a rebuke. In those instances, if anyone said to her 'Come here!' she would be startled and say at once: 'I'll fix it. I'll do whatever you want'. Poor Dilber! She only felt at ease after hearing the words 'You didn't do anything wrong' and seeing her masters' kind treatment.

Dilber's mistress was always kind to her. She was taught to treat everyone with kindness after all. But no act of kindness could hide her low opinion of female slaves, an opinion she had inherited from her Egyptian family. Dilber, having already suffered cruelty and degradation at the hands of humanity, could recognize the belittling, loathing look on her mistress's face.[8] This humiliation would manifest itself in the mistress's seemingly forgiving and understanding demeanour towards the female slaves. For instance, she would pardon the slaves for their little mistakes, only to say: 'What do you expect? Just a slave girl, after all!' And these words, this demeaning forgiveness, inflicted as much pain on Dilber as any beating would have.

But perhaps what humiliated Dilber the most was being subjected to Celal Bey's capricious demands. Celal Bey had turned her into a plaything. And this manipulative artist's ever-changing, childish whims and desires deeply hurt Dilber's sense of dignity. Indeed, this dolorous creature had become a plaything for the young, admired, exalted and fortunate master of noble character. Some days, he would dress her up as an ancient Egyptian, adorn her hair with flowers and place her in a

[8] Ottoman families, similar to Sezai's own, relocated from Egypt to Istanbul in the aftermath of Muhammad Ali Pasha's death in the nineteenth century. In Istanbul, these families became notable for their opulent lifestyle, extravagant spending and grand mansions populated by a workforce of domestic slaves.

room. He would then open the windows overlooking the sea, and make a painting of Dilber, fully embellished and bejewelled against the reflection of the soul-inspiring colours of the sun, setting in a pink and blue haze on the horizon of the Marmara Sea. Dilber was made to sit for hours before this 'Roman' statue, cold and unswayed by any emotion, while he would constantly order Dilber about: 'Don't move! Don't touch the flowers!' In moments of frustration with his work, he would even go so far as to tell her not to breathe. In response to these intimidations, Dilber would only shake her head in exasperation, and, like a queen exiled to boredom in a distant corner of her palace, she would sometimes allow a quiet 'Oh, my God' to escape her lips.

The comfort and safety of this house had undoubtedly contributed to Dilber's burgeoning beauty over the past few months. Her body was transforming. She was getting taller, and her complexion had acquired a graceful and youthful glow, pleasing to the eye.

On summer days, usually in the early afternoons, she would grab a French novel and seclude herself in the gazebo. To enjoy her solitude, she would hide herself from prying eyes and sit in the most secret corner of this emerald chamber, enclosed by acacia trees, and read *Paul et Virginie*, while the birds perched on the branches of the surrounding trees, stretching their necks as if to watch her, their songs hovering above her head, creating a beautiful and harmonious ambiance.[9]

'Oh, how happy is this little Virginie!' she would think to herself as she turned the pages.

Dilber thought that being the slave of a rather haughty Egyptian mistress and a plaything in the hands of a cheerful, self-absorbed master was the biggest fortune of her life. Deep in her heart, however, Dilber craved a passionate love, like that of Virginie's. But the tragic destiny of Virginie, how Paul watched her get crushed by and then disappear into the wild sky-high waves, would upset her, and a few tears always fell on the pages of her book.

On yet another early afternoon, when the sunshine cascaded down to earth and turned everything into fire, Dilber retreated to her usual tranquil corner. This gazebo was her only refuge. Here, she felt as if she were all by herself. Encircled by the cool shade of acacia trees, the happy melodies of the birds and the fragrance of the blossoms, it was protected from all the tumult and sorrow of the world, worthy of being called the secret home

[9] *Paul et Virginie* (1788) by Bernardin de Saint-Pierre, depicting the tragic love story of two island children, emerged as one of the nineteenth-century Ottoman Empire's most beloved novels, translated twice before the turn of the century.

of a fairy. When she was in this gazebo, Dilber felt that she could be like all other young girls her age. She could be coy or playful and appreciate beautiful things.

That day, she was softly humming a tune and adorning her hair with flowers, looking just like the girl on that painting that she had admired in Celal Bey's room. In the meantime, Celal Bey was searching for Dilber. After over half an hour of looking around the house and being unable to find Dilber, Celal Bey decided to step out into the garden. He called her name repeatedly: 'Dilber, Dilber!' Though she heard him, she did not respond. Celal Bey's search for Dilber, his plaything, grew ever more frantic as he kept looking for her everywhere.

Right when Celal Bey passed by the gazebo, a pleasant north-westerly wind blew and gently stirred the branches of the acacia trees, revealing the secret hiding place of this little fugitive, this mischievous recluse. Never one to leave her alone, Celal Bey quickly made his way over to Dilber, laughed heartily at the flower chaplet adorning her head and said: 'Come on Cleopatra, let's go!'

Poor Cleopatra, she was the captive of this Alexander who dragged her against her will to the courtyard. Celal had already planned a pose for her that day. He would have her lean her back against a marble column and put on her a dress that had been patched in many places, torn and ripped near her arms and breasts. That's how he wanted to paint her. But Dilber refused:

'No! No! There is no way I will wear this', she told Celal Bey while holding the collars of her garment tightly with both hands.

'But please, Cleopatra'.

'No, I don't want to, I said, I don't want to…'

Celal pressed his hands – strong enough to break any plaything – on Dilber's shoulders and dressed her up against her will. He then went to his corner and began a dramatic painting of a beggar girl.[10] Dilber stood there in her ripped costume. Her spotless, flawless ivory arms were exposed; her pinkish white, dawn-coloured bosom was barely covered. Her tousled pitch-black hair fell on her back and on her naked body. Alas! Dilber had failed to defend herself. She leaned her head against the ancient column, feeling powerless and weak and wept softly. Tears! What an accomplishment for Celal… The tears of the model posing as a beggar girl contributed as much to the success of the artwork as the strokes of the

[10] Both Jean-Léon Gérôme's *Jeune fille du Caire* (1873) and the Eastern beauty trope in nineteenth-century Orientalist paintings may have influenced Sezai when depicting Celal's positioning of Dilber as a beggar girl in this scene. See Figure 15.

artist's brush. These arms... These arms that looked like pillars of light opening the rose-coloured gates of dawn towards a crystalline sky on a sweet spring morning... Shoulders coming down in such subtle curves... That bosom... Only ancient Greek marble statues that stood the test of time with their vitality and charm could be as beautiful. Astonishing! Who could have imagined that, in the brief span of two comfortable years

Figure 15 Jean-Léon Gérôme, *Jeune fille du Caire* (1873). Courtesy of Sotheby's.

between fifteen and seventeen, when the human form and complexion, especially in young girls, change most profoundly, Dilber's beauty would gain such power and distinction?

Celal, this grand artist, set his brush aside and rested his arm on his knee. His fingers were entwined in his hair. His eyes, accustomed to beauty, were fixed in wonder on the beggar girl in dishevelled clothes, weeping quietly before him. One minute… Three minutes… Six minutes… Dilber was still crying. She felt so conscious of her slavery and so deeply humiliated by it. It was her slavery which had delivered her to the endless caprices of those who had prosperity and wealth, leaving her sad and heartbroken.

Celal could see in her languid eyes and thin, curled lips the sorrow of her unfulfilled, ardent passions, her yearning to be loved and respected as a woman. At that moment, he recalled that Dilber had no mother on whose bosom she could cry, no father or brothers to protect her. And he tried to imagine the exploitation, the cruelty and the humiliation that she endured in her life of enslavement. Her innocent desires… Her modest hopes and wishes… All in all, the entire history of this girl, abandoned by humanity, passed in front of Celal's eyes and overwhelmed him with sorrow. He rose from his chair and said: 'I beg for your forgiveness, Cleopatra. If you so desire, I'll break this brush. Here, I am asking you to forgive me. I apologise to you. Why are you still crying?'

Dilber eventually calmed down. Then, without saying a word, she put her clothes back on and went outside. But those eyes… that bosom… those lips… those tears streaming from her sad, loving eyes into his soul; they left Celal, that stoic statue, in utter and restless turmoil. Thus far in life, his biggest point of pride and satisfaction was to live bravely and with fortitude. Having always been a figure of confidence and exuberance, he had now found himself alone in the room, searching his heart for answers and wrestling with unfamiliar emotions. He placed his trembling, cold hands on his fiery forehead, burning up with the flames of this newly kindled romance, and he was lost in his thoughts. As he went up the stairs, he was asking himself: 'Why has this plaything affected me so deeply?'

Dilber's beauty left Celal Bey shaken. For days he remained lost in thought, and at night he lay awake, trying to soothe his heart. Until recently, Celal had teased Dilber at every chance, but it was different now. Whenever he was in Dilber's presence, he became pensive and quiet and secretly watched her with an affectionate gaze. Dilber was no longer a plaything for Celal. His Cleopatra was turning into a Juliet. As days of doubt followed one another, Celal wrestled with conflicting thoughts. But once he surfaced from the depths of these stormy reflections, he found himself racing towards a bright horizon, a new realm of love that was opening up in front of his eyes. What a baffling transformation this was! Everything appeared different to him now! On quiet nights, when one could almost hear the silent footsteps of fairies tiptoeing through poetic thoughts and romantic dreams, he lay wide awake until dawn, sleepless with uncertainty and wonder, deprived of the much needed, embalming solace of sleep.

One such night, lying awake in bed and tormented by doubts of love, he suddenly rose and exclaimed: 'Once more'. Yes, he was going to see Dilber one more time. He wanted to know whether his feelings were real. For all his life, he had admired only the idealised beauty of ancient Greek goddesses, preserved in their universally admired statues. But now, he felt betrayed by his hard-to-please eyes. He wished to get rid of his doubts, persuade his heart and thus ease his nerves and pain.

He began to dress himself. Seized by a thought that dawned upon him in a moment of fervour, he rushed downstairs to Dilber's bedroom. Yet, when he reached her door, he hesitated. Flutters… Oh, those flutters that accompany every first step of love! They sapped the strength from his hands, kept him from turning the door handle and forced his longing heart to pause. His mind was flooded with thoughts: To come into a young girl's room in the middle of the night; to be at the door of her bedroom guarded only by honour and dignity; to enter the privacy of her palace of chastity; and to violate this purest and most sacred rule like a bandit… This was a crime! In that instant, in that blinding darkness, he felt an intense sense of shame, and his conscience stared back at him with wrathful eyes. He covered his face with his arm and shivered at the thought of taking advantage of this slave girl whose body and health were burdened with unbearable manual labour; whose chaste bed was rendered unprotected and vulnerable to any violation. With these thoughts he retreated from the door. Alas! Because the irresistible power of love suddenly flooded his mind and shook these thoughts at their very core, Celal Bey entered the room just to admire her beauty and to stand in awe before a Mary-like chastity, and he stopped at the head of her bed.

It was with these sentiments that he entered the room. He stood by her bed; she was asleep. There was a candle by her bedside, almost burnt down. The way she was sleeping on her back, in a deep slumber, made her look frail. A few wrinkles around her eyes, illuminated by the light of the oil lamp, revealed the secret sufferings of this young heart. Her eyelashes, the charming shadows of her loving eyes, were wet. She must have cried. At that moment, behind Dilber's tousled hair, something caught Celal's eyes. He looked at it closely in astonishment, with appraising eyes. A photograph! But whose photograph was this? Could he take a closer look, just once? But why? It seemed unconscionable to him that he could unravel what was perhaps a poor slave girl's most precious memento, her most sacred secret. Perhaps it was the picture of her only source of consolation in life, her mother? Or her father? Or her lover? This last thought devastated his already suffering and overwrought mind and took away his remaining strength. He grabbed the picture and held it under the oil lamp which cast a poetic light on this sleeping girl. He froze, and his face turned white. This was his picture! Though he wished to fall on his knees and cry at her feet, he refrained from doing so, fearing that he might awake her and that his presence there in the middle of the night would offend her. Instead, he left the picture in its place and returned to his room. Once in his bed, for the first time in twenty-three years, tears streamed from his once-indifferent eyes.

Chapter 7

It was the thirteenth day of the Arabic month.[1] After a hot and long summer day, the family had come together for dinner in the early evening hours, under the green canopy of tall trees. Two of Asaf Pasha's nieces had also joined them that evening. The pasha's daughter Tesliye, however, could not be at the table with everyone else. She had a minor cold, but her mother, in her persistent and overbearing ways, had insisted that she stay in her room, thus ruining Tesliye's mood. As moonlight flickered through the leaves and fell on the white tablecloth, there was only one thing everyone talked about at the dinner table: Tesliye's forthcoming marriage to a prosperous and wealthy pasha.

One of Asaf Pasha's nieces was also at the table. She was wearing a long, light-blue dress, styled after the latest Parisian fashion, and three strands of pearls around her neck. In this costume, she looked not merely like a vision borne of eastern fancy, but more like a sky dotted with waning morning stars. Asaf Pasha's nieces had had an eventful day on their way to his mansion and, even before unpinning their veils, had begun to complain about how they had been treated by the women on the ferry. They told everyone how they had been unable to find a private cabin and therefore had to sit among other women in the common area. There, they had faced the scrutinising gaze of these women, whose envy was surely fuelled by misery and poverty. The women had attacked the young sisters rather rudely, criticising with their sharp tongues their new-style veils, their *ferace*s, how they dressed and even how they

[1] Sezai did not specify in either of the two editions to which of the twelve months in the Islamic Hijri calendar he was referring.

walked.[2] They had even raised their voices and created a scene in front of everyone.

'Look at these women! Ah, friends, look what the world has come to!' they yelled. The younger sister was particularly shaken by the experience. 'Stepping out on the street is not safe!' she had said wrathfully, reddening in dismay. Hers was the kind of intense disdain that lends women the utmost beauty whenever their Mary-like chastity is attacked. Indeed, that day, while she and her sister were getting off the ferry, a couple of men had openly expressed their interest in her, using a kind of language that she had never heard under her father's upbringing.

We must admit how contradictory it is to insult these virtuous women, veiled in the name of public morality and manners and then to defend veiling to Europeans by saying that it shows our respect for virtuous women. Nowadays, there's a particular group of young men whose mere existence is a disgrace to our country. These young men, with their canary-yellow cravats, their light-coloured jackets, their rather thick black piping and their blue trousers, dare to assault women, thereby assaulting public morality.[3] Just as they think they can attack respectable folks whom they have never met, so they attack literary works about which they know nothing. Indeed, their utmost praise of belles-lettres is reserved for either nit-pickers or critics who only know how to curse, condemn, or vituperate. Their vulgarity is so competent, so refined, that they would evoke envy in the most miserable and lowly members in society – those who,

[2] The *ferace*, worn by both men and women, is a loose long coat with wide arms. In the nineteenth century, women's *ferace*s underwent significant transformations, influenced by European fashion trends. These changes resulted in *ferace*s that featured lighter colours, intricate decoration and a slimmer cut. The critique voiced by the women on the ferry primarily concerned the nieces' European-inspired *ferace*s, which in 1870 also prompted the government to enact a set of regulations to address this fashion shift.

[3] The sartorial choices criticised here are emblematic of the *alafranga züppe* or westernised dandy, a character-type that became prominent in nineteenth-century Ottoman literature. This figure, often depicted as a young Ottoman man who wrongly adopted western ways, was critiqued for his ostentatious European-style clothing. Notable representations of this character include Ahmet Mithat Efendi's *Felatun Bey and Rakım Efendi* (1875) and Hüseyin Rahmi Gürpınar's *Şık* (Chic, 1889). Gürpınar, in the introduction of his 1908 novel *Şıpsevdi* (Quick to Love), has categorised three types of *alafranga* dandies: those from distinguished families educated in French and Europe, those married to western women living in Beyoğlu, and the dandies who are often subjects of ridicule in literature for their exaggerated attire. Gürpınar's critique has focused on this third group, whose fashion choices, 'whether concerning tightness, looseness, shortness, length, thinness, or thickness, transcend all conventional standards of taste and custom; they defy any measure of reason, always exceeding the bounds of normality'. Sezai's criticism targets this third type of *alafranga* dandy.

deprived of the light of education and decency, dwell perpetually in darkness of poverty and ignorance. They think that glory, fame, excellency and victory all belong to those who spit ink at the face of genius, like a venom-spitting snake, or who offer the most articulate insults. Their fingertips have yellowed from smoking cigarettes from morning till night; their stooping backs are hunched from walking on uneven streets in their neighbourhoods; or from stooping to write clean copies of their drafts at their offices; and from bowing to greet people, as courtesy demands. Excessive drinking and their poor lifestyle have given their complexion a greyish hue. In their tiny black eyes, one can see how evil and deceit have replaced education and merit. And yet, they are under the impression that all women are captivated and charmed by their sense of fashion, the grace of their figures and their manners and good breeding. God help those who would wish to approach these pompous men who have barely enough eloquence to compose letters and manage to publish a work or two (all of which read worse than their letters). They favourably mention Lamartine, whom they know only by name, and they find Hugo, whom they know only from pictures, worthy of praise. Heaven forbid that someone decent and humble dares to critique them on the topic of morality and manners, the two gatekeepers of national pride! They would fly into a rage and put on a haughty and triumphant attitude, like Alexander the Great addressing an emperor he's about to conquer, and say: 'I'll show him the power of my pen!' One cannot help but wonder what they would possibly do next. Probably they would pen flawless profanities made with mediocre wordplays. Dear reader, forgive us, for we have digressed from our story, but we were upset about how these two young women, two rare models of beauty and virtue, were attacked by dishonourable men whose only literary merit, virtue and weapon of victory is profanities. Now we shall return to our story.

The topic of Tesliye's forthcoming wedding had brought a broad smile on Zehra Hanım's face, for she, like all women, harboured in her heart an ambition for prosperity, a desire for distinction and a love of bragging. Zehra Hanım often dreamed about a bride for her only son, who, though young, was already graced with both a big fortune and exceptional talent. In her dreams, this ideal bride was the daughter of one of Istanbul's illustrious families, a family whose wealth and nobility were the talk of the entire city. Yet Zehra Hanım's aspirations did not end there; driven by a fervent desire to climb the social ladder, she would sometimes allow her ambitions to soar even further.

While Zehra Hanım was occupied by these thoughts and dreams at the table, she noticed that her son was not his usual cheerful and joyful self.

He had not touched the food in front of him, and for the last three or four minutes, he seemed to have been lost in thought. After closely examining her son with probing motherly eyes that see through all secrets, Zehra Hanım began to speak, her voice sharp enough to snap him out of his trance:

'Celal, did you congratulate your sister and give her a kiss on the eyes? Such a fortunate marriage this is…'

'Maybe you should ask her about that'.

'Why should I ask her? Aren't nobility and fortune all one needs for a marriage?'

'No, dear mother. It is beauty and virtue… Love mostly follows from those two'.

'And are nobility and fortune impediments to any of this? In my opinion, if a man does not possess power, skills, wealth, or any nobility that is worth mentioning in public, then marrying him solely for the sake of his looks is quite banal. And besides, isn't compatibility between characters what is most desired in a marriage? Is it possible for two people, one raised as upper class and the other coming from the lower ranks of society, to get along well? How could we expect someone raised in poverty and with neglect to be worthy of a young man or a girl of noble upbringing? How could they ever be happy if one of them constantly felt as if his reputation and fortune were being pulled down, while the other's pride was hurt?'

'But aren't there souls that shine with purity and loftiness even in the midst of poverty and misery, just as stars shine in darkness? Does a heart truly need wealth and nobility to fall in love? I believe that the truest fortune in life is nothing but a pair of beautiful eyes that reflect a beautiful soul; the greatest wealth is nothing but a heartfelt smile that shines on rose-coloured lips. Can there be a nobility on earth greater than beauty, or wealth greater than a pure heart?'

Zehra Hanım turned to the other guests at the table and said: 'I wouldn't ever want noble people to become artists or poets. Their unrealistic ideas may lower their social status and dignity in the eyes of the public'.

Celal responded: 'Nobility worships vanity and wealth, wealth worships spectacles of nobility. I, however, worship virtue and love'.

Zehra Hanım, slightly perturbed, replied: 'Celal, I don't appreciate your ideas about wealth and nobility'.

'Perhaps they're all wrong. But even so, these are my ideas and beliefs. I think one should never lie to anyone, especially not to God and their mothers'.

Asaf Pasha refrained from joining the conversation between his wife and his son and instead conversed with his nieces.

Chapter 7

As it often happens at the end of dinner parties, a general feeling of happiness spilled from the table. These joyful sounds and the bursts of laughter reverberated in the air, reaching Dilber, who was waiting outside Miss Tesliye's room, gripped by the melancholy of the lonely. Each echo of joy from the dinner party deeply resonated within her soul already consumed by a powerful emotion, a secret love. She listened to the laughter of young men and women at the table, who were incontestably proud of their nobility and wealth, and elated with happiness. Theirs was the kind of laughter marked by secure futures and prosperous destinies. And here was Dilber, at the threshold of her mistress's bedroom, waiting. She felt irresolute with the love of a man just like them, noble and wealthy, and realised what a cruel penance it was for slaves to have a heart and a soul. Bereft, she wept.

They had all left the dinner table and were happily strolling along the trees by the pond under the moonlight. Zehra Hanım watched her son from afar, then approached him and asked: 'Celal, have you quit smoking?' Celal, startled as if awakened from a dream, replied: 'No, I simply forgot to bring it'.

Sensing the unease in his casual response, Zehra Hanım knew that something was not right. Her only son, her flesh and blood, whom she had raised with so much sacrifice, was hiding something from her. Fearing the devastation of future tragedies that might befall her son and no longer able to endure the uncertainty, she chose to believe that a mother's love granted her every right, even the claim to know the deepest secrets of her child's heart. She felt weary, overwhelmed by these uneasy thoughts, and decided to go upstairs to check on her daughter. When she arrived there, Dilber was sitting on a chair by the door. As soon as she saw her mistress, she stood up. They began to talk.

'Did you cry?'

'No, ma'am'.

'Then why are your eyes all red?'

'I don't know, ma'am'.

Zehra Hanım didn't dwell too much on Dilber's words. She talked to her daughter for a little while, and afterwards the entire family took a carriage ride to the Fener neighbourhood for an outing. A couple of hours after their return home, everyone retreated to their bedroom. But it was only Celal Bey who could not fall asleep. Just as the rising sun awakens the eyes, the dispersing light of the amorous moon made sleep impossible for this young, ardent soul. He could not sleep. He sat in his bed and grabbed a book, hoping that it would calm his heart and soothe his suffering soul. He read for an hour, yet he didn't understand a word of what he had read. Restless and sleepless, he checked the time: It was almost dawn. He decided to go down to the garden to watch the sunrise. He put on his clothes and quietly went down the stairs, careful not to wake anyone. At the bottom of the stairs, he noticed someone looking out the window melancholically, deep in thought. 'Who could it be?' he wondered. He approached the figure with reservation and fear. It was Dilber! It looked as if she, too, could not sleep, for she was still wearing the same dress from the day before. They started to talk to each other.

'Look how the stars over there are shining on this quiet night', Celal Bey said. 'The Gemini twins over the horizon, facing the direction of your heart. Don't you think they look like two white doves flying towards the horizon, to tell Venus what's on their mind? They are beautiful. They are all so beautiful. But you, you are more beautiful than all the stars. Tell me, why couldn't you sleep?'

At first, Dilber wanted to hide her true feelings and simply say: 'No reason, sir. I did actually sleep'. But before she could say anything, Celal saw it all in her eyes, for Dilber's eyes were incapable of keeping secrets.

'Do you know how much you mean to me?' he asked her. 'You are the reason why I am lost in thought during the day and wide awake at night'.

They both averted their eyes from each other and instead looked down for a minute. The young lovers were in a trance, throwing quick, covetous glances at each other and quietly revealing the affection and surprise in their hearts. Celal Bey nervously suggested that they go out into the garden, so they went down the stairs and headed out to the garden. What a sudden turn of events this was! As they walked side by side, in their new-found intimacy, they kept telling each other to be cautious with a 'Hush!' or 'Quiet!' or 'Don't step over there!' Whenever there was a creak on the stairs or their clothes brushed against something and disturbed the deep silence of the night, they acted as if it were a rumble that would wake the entire household. And whenever the faintest of sounds resonated in the air, so faint that even those still awake in the courtyard could not hear, they immediately paused to see if they had awakened anyone. Thus, after meticulous cautiousness, they finally made it to the garden. A cool breeze fell from the leaves and wafted through the flowers, playing with Dilber's hair and filling the hearts of the two young people with a shiver.

They sat side by side, timidly, on an ivy-covered garden wall, seeing it as a refuge for their love. There was not a sound to be heard, nor a soul moving, only the stars above their heads flickered in the eternity of the heavens. Celal Bey held Dilber's hands. 'Are you cold?' he asked.

'This gentle breeze is the breath of the flowers. You won't get cold, will you?'

'No', Dilber replied. 'It is not the breeze that touches me. It is this view, this grandeur'.

In the meantime, hues of light-blue announced the approaching sunrise to the lovers. Dilber and Celal saw around them the beauty of nature and in each other's eyes the beauty of creation. As they exchanged vows of love and loyalty, the stars in the east were entranced in front of the distant smiles of the approaching dawn, their colours fading. After watching over the lovers all night, the stars began to disappear one by one. The two lovers walked through the garden gate and began to follow a path taken over by trees and plants, barely seeing where they were going.

Midway through, they stopped by a lonely grave, enclosed by a small fence and illuminated by a bright star on cloudless nights. Celal pointed to the freshly covered grave. He said: 'Beneath this earth lies an eighteen-year-old girl. She was engaged to a young man who was adored by the people of this village. For years, she waited for him to marry her, and in the end this young man abandoned her and married someone else, and thus this grave'. After they said a prayer for the deceased girl, the two walked up the highest hill nearby. Celal Bey seated Dilber in a meadow surrounded by budding flowers. As he sat at her feet, Dilber's face, more beautiful than all the spring blossoms, was the only thing visible to Cemal through the grass and flowers.

The eastern sky gradually brightened. Although the earth still remained shrouded in darkness, the sky had begun to lighten with a dark, bluish glow. To hide their throne of love from strangers' eyes, the darkness of the night draped them like a black curtain, and the sky above their heads sparkled like a crown of good fortune. Just then the rays of sun spread through the sky like a rainbow, and all of a sudden the eastern sky, until then veiled by feathery clouds, turned into a rosy pink. As the rays of sun flickered on that transparent veil in the distance, it looked as if the secrets of the universe, the mysteries of the heavens appeared beyond the horizon.

The fog that had descended on the waters of the Sea of Marmara at night had taken on a red hue at dawn and then quickly dissipated. Once the rosy-fingered dawn lifted the sparkling red veil from their beautiful faces, the Princes' Islands appeared on the still waters of the Sea of Marmara, each standing like a Greek goddess. There was something poetic about the mist. As it disappeared into the rising sun, it resembled the long celestial skirts of angels floating in the sky fleeing to the heavens. Over there, in the distance, in the most secluded, most secretive corners of the forest, impenetrable by the sun – unless it changed and refracted its light – hundreds of birds sang an intoxicating love song as these two lovers' lips were locked in a kiss for more than a minute, filling their hearts with endless love.

How many moments and seconds in this world are worthy of being immortalised? Up in the sky, the colours of dawn; down on earth, a gold-dipped morning, a bridal chamber covered with flowers, the first kiss cheered by the melodies of the birds… Aren't all of these worthy of being immortalised? An ephemeral smile that only surfaces when one is absorbed in dreams; a smile that all words fail to describe… Isn't that smile also worthy of being immortalised?

Ah, poor memory! How it relentlessly tries to survive in human flesh, a heap of dust that we feel perishing with every passing day. It holds on to a melancholy gaze for years… It hangs on to a word, a smile, for decades. It tries to capture all memories and sorrows that pass by at a dizzying speed. When it loses all its strength and endurance with this colossal task, all our hopes for the future vanish. At that moment, the past that ushers along our lives is wrecked in a sea of oblivion. Then, like a fatally wounded soldier, it abandons its post and leaves us at the foot of the grave.

Chapter 8

The sun was up. Zehra Hanım had already been to her son's room three times to check on him, but Celal wasn't in his room. His bed cover was on the floor, a book was left open on the nightstand, a candle that must have flickered all night had burnt all the way to its wick, and clothes were scattered all around the room. Zehra Hanım watched this scene with a heavy heart. The room was no doubt a reflection of her son's state of mind.

Zehra Hanım checked Dilber's room as well, four times to be exact. Dilber was not in her room either. This cannot be a coincidence, she thought to herself. Her motherly heart, already in turmoil because of her son's contemplative mood, had now stumbled upon a new revelation. Suddenly, she realised that the palace of fortune whose gates she had pushed open with such ambition and desire were fast closing into her face; she could see that the name and reputation that she desperately wanted might now be abandoning her forever. The mysterious disappearance of these two young people, she thought to herself, had to have something to do with the affairs of the heart. And it suddenly dawned on her that love must be the force behind Celal's transformation. How his joy and vivacity had been replaced by lovesickness, she thought, and how her son's old quick-witted and energetic self had recently left its place to pensive silence.

This was too much to bear. How could her son worship a creature who Zehra Hanım doubted could even be called human; a slave that she deemed unworthy of having any rights in society. When the truth about her son's feelings towards Dilber struck her like lightning, she lost her footing, stumbled and leaned against the wall, overcome by a sudden faintness. The female slaves flocked to their mistress and carried Zehra Hanım to her room. A while later, after the commotion had subsided,

Zehra Hanım gathered everyone and warned them not to say a word about any of this to Celal or Dilber.

Zehra Hanım was adamant about not accepting anyone into her room. On an ordinary day, her husband, Asaf Pasha, would not visit the harem section of his house, for he had entrusted the running of the harem entirely to his wife. But that day, he came to the harem as soon as he heard about Zehra Hanım's sudden illness.

'What's the matter? I heard you've suddenly fallen ill this morning, is that true? Your hands are freezing'.

'You know how worried I was about Celal and the recent change in his mood and demeanour. Now I see that it was all because he fell for a slave girl'.

'How do you mean, a slave girl?'

'Dilber'.

'This is not possible! After we invested so much time and effort in his education and right when we were about to arrange a prosperous marriage for him, is he going to leave everything, all our efforts, his future, in a slave's dirty hands, soiled with labour? This is not possible!'

'They've both been missing from their rooms since this morning'.

'Without a question we must urgently rectify this situation. One cannot sacrifice years of experience, a lifetime of wise and rational decisions for the transient madness of fleeting youthful passion… Why do you worry yourself sick? Ban them from seeing each other and chastise them both!'

'You leave that to me. And don't say a word to Celal!'

Asaf Pasha left the room, visibly upset and agitated. In the meantime, Celal and Dilber were returning from their hiding place in nature – at times a nest of flowers, at others a place where beauty revealed itself in abundance. As they entered the garden, the two lovers were struck with surprise and sorrow by how swiftly the joyful hours had slipped away in love's sweet absent-mindedness.

Once they arrived home, Celal Bey had to get ready for an event. He was invited to spend the night at his uncle's *yalı* on the Bosphorus.[1] To make it to the ferry on time, Celal hurried upstairs and changed. In the hallway, he ran into a slave girl, and the following conversation took place between them:

'Is my mother in her room?'

'Yes, master. The mistress did not sleep well last night, so she's resting now'.

[1] *Yalı*, an originally Greek word meaning 'coast', is used to describe wooden waterfront mansions on the Bosphorus shores, built by Ottoman nobles and foreign ambassadors.

'Bring my cane. I'll go see her'.

'No, master. They gave orders. Nobody is allowed in her room. Even the young ladies left without seeing her'.

'She isn't ill, is she?'

'No, my master. She's fine'.

Celal Bey did not suspect anything, so when the slave girl told him that his mother was fine, he followed up on his plan and quickly left the house for the ferry. Not an inkling of doubt or suspicion stirred in the hearts of these two lovesick, inexperienced souls, completely blinded by their emotions.

The ferry left the pier. In Celal Bey's eyes, everything seemed brighter and livelier that day. How could it not; how could he not notice more beauty around him after treasuring the beautiful face of his beloved for hours? As the ferry sailed on, he felt eternity opening before his eyes on the horizon of the Marmara Sea. After he had changed ferries at the Galata Bridge, the Bosphorus presented yet another magnificent panorama. As Celal sailed through this spectacular scenery, he discovered places that he had never noticed before, places that promised such tranquil beauty, enough to bless two lovers with eternal happiness. He felt such sublime sensations in his heart, feelings to which he had never before paid attention. He imagined those grand waterfront mansions as a nest where the two lovers might live happily ever after. It was as if the sky were holding a mirror, showing his beloved's face everywhere, and the breeze felt as pleasant as his beloved's locks brushing against his face. Alas! While fate was caressing Celal with sweet dreams, it was in fact preparing him for a dreadful tragedy. For who can stand in the way of fate? Do not all lofty human thoughts, all wisdom, all catastrophes, even the day of judgment itself, tremble in submission before it? Poor young man! He did not know that fate had already delivered his beloved into the cruel hands of those indifferent to the human heart.

Chapter 9

How tragic it is that people don't always act virtuously in the case of crimes that aren't yet forbidden by law. This is perhaps due to the prevalence of social ills, more specifically, a lack of good manners, widespread ignorance and superstitions that prevent moral and compassionate behaviour. It is rare to see people follow the commands and prohibitions of their conscience and act with moral integrity and kindness. Zehra Hanım was no exception to this.

It was nighttime. Zehra Hanım had retreated into a quiet corner in her room and was anxiously waiting for a visitor to arrive. She looked mentally and physically tormented and kept inquiring why the much-anticipated visitor had not yet arrived. No one truly knew the reason, though they speculated it was a fire in the area. 'Perhaps it's close to where she lives', they suggested to the mistress, but even this did little to alleviate Zehra Hanım's growing unease.

Zehra Hanım had found herself in a most difficult position. She knew that within a few hours she would have to resolve a grave dilemma: whether to sacrifice her son's future, already jeopardised by the passions and illusions of youth and the happiness promised to her as his mother, or to destroy this worthless slave who stood in the way of their happiness and prosperity? Zehra Hanım descended from one of those Egyptian families in Istanbul known for their deep contempt toward ill-fated slaves. She also was a woman of vanity, in love with the European life of pomp and nobility, driven by ambition and hunger for wealth and status. In the end, all of these reasons led her to the decision to sell Dilber.

Just as she had made up her mind about her plan, the door opened. A woman entered, her stout body wrapped in a long, stitched cardigan that fell to her feet, covering her big belly. Above her disproportionately big, round cheeks sat small and slanted eyes, giving away her Tatar heritage.

Her imploring eyes emanated a forced charm. She walked in with an insincere smile, revealing her remaining few teeth as she uttered compliments and prayers.

When the woman entered the room, she found Zehra Hanım reclining on the sofa, resting her head on her hand. Zehra Hanım's furrowed brows revealed the strength of her determination, and yet her lips were quivering, like rose petals caught in the autumn wind, foreboding the dire decision that she was about to declare. A lamp in the corner, veiled with black tulle, cast a weak light that accentuated the darkness of the room. Outside the windows, in the distance, the fire in the city was picking up in intensity, the reflection of the flames pervading the room. In their glow, Zehra Hanım resembled a Roman empress. The flickering reflection of the flames had taken on a breathtaking grace as they danced on her jewel-in-a-crown-like blonde hair, her fair skin, dark-blue eyes and beautiful lips, lending her an eerie beauty. However, as soon as the slave trader woman walked in, Zehra Hanım shook off the heavy load of her tormented soul with a voice that resonated in the room like thunder and said: 'This Dilber you brought into my house. She is staining the honour of my house, ruining the future of my son. Tomorrow, you will take her back to where you got her'.

The slave trader woman considered herself to be rather special for having received such an order from the mistress and knew that it would serve her financial interest well to execute it. Laughing loudly, she said: 'Ah, my lady! Don't you even worry about such a small thing! Tomorrow, I'll take her off your hands and find her a proper home'.

'Very early tomorrow, you understand?' Zehra Hanım sharply said to the slave trader. 'Now, leave me alone'. After the slave trader had left, Zehra Hanım was all by herself in the room. She walked to the window and for a while stood there, contemplating. By the time she walked back and collapsed onto the sofa, her eyes, misty with an unknown, secret emotion, looked like dew-covered violets.

Chapter 10

Çaresaz, a Circassian slave girl, who shared a room with Dilber, spent the night talking about the Caucasus and captivity, weeping inconsolably all the while. The grief that stirred her very being lent her voice a power, giving her words a strange and haunting simplicity and beauty. And this wasn't lost on Dilber. Sad to see her dear friend, her fellow slave, in this unusual state, Dilber asked: 'Why are you crying?'

'No reason', Çaresaz replied. 'Crying is the biggest right a slave has. We have that freedom, no?' she uttered. This was rather odd! Who could have broken poor Çaresaz's heart so deeply that, even after Dilber undressed and slipped into the bed, she was still crying. But there was no way that Dilber could fall asleep when her friend was crying, so she got up and started talking to Çaresaz:

'Çaresaz! Tears shed alone are bitter. You have never kept any secrets from me before, so why are you not telling me what upset you now? Are you homesick? Or did you remember crying in your mother's arms as a child? If you don't open your heart to me, who do you think here will have mercy on you, the mistresses in the house? And who will cry for you, the masters?'

'Oh, no, no!' Çaresaz said. 'In their eyes, a slave who cries deserves nothing but beatings and punishment. How could there be any heart or compassion in those masters who force ill slaves out of their beds to serve – because they think we fake our pain and illness. Don't tell me that they have mercy'.

Çaresaz gave her friend a hug and a few kisses and said: 'My dear sister, I know you have a tender heart. I know you're feeling sorry for me… But believe me, it's nothing. I'll calm down in a moment and go to bed. Don't you worry. It's nothing!' After this conversation, both girls climbed into their beds.

Chapter 10

It was not fully dawn yet when a woman entered their room and woke Dilber.

'What do you want from me?' Dilber asked her.

'Get up', the woman told Dilber. 'Put your things in a bag. Put your veil on. There's no future for you in this house'.

Dishevelled and bewildered, Dilber stood at the foot of her bed and rubbed her eyes. Puzzled by what was happening, she asked Çaresaz: 'What is she saying? I don't understand!' For this naive mind could not grasp that the joy of just two days earlier could be followed by such a ruinous future. This cold-hearted woman stood by Dilber's bedside like a prison guard taking a condemned prisoner to her execution. 'Hurry up, we must leave this house before morning. Such is the order of the masters!' she kept telling Dilber.

The woman stood there motionless, as Dilber pulled her veil and *ferace* from the drawer and pinned up her hair in front of the mirror. In the corner, Çaresaz was sobbing. There were no tears in Dilber's eyes, but her complexion was as pale as her white veil. She put on her *ferace* and walked towards the door. Çaresaz caught up with her, and after looking into each other's eyes for a brief moment, the two embraced. The coldness on Dilber's face caused a slight quivering on her friend's lips.

As Dilber went down to the garden with the slave trader trailing behind her, the trader noticed Dilber's empty hands and asked: 'Where's your bag, girl?' Dilber had remained silent until then, but now she responded firmly: 'I don't want it!'

Despite Dilber's firm refusal to take any of her belongings, the slave trader went back upstairs and grabbed Dilber's bag, hoping to claim the items for herself. As she was about to leave the room, Çaresaz stopped her. She pulled off a ring from her finger and, choked by her sobbing, begged: 'Give this to Dilber for me'.

The birds were singing in their morning grace and gaiety in the garden that, just the day before, Dilber had called a joyful paradise. Yet now, frozen, numb, unable to muster the strength to think or breathe, she stood there, looking ghastly pale, like the Venus statue in the garden.

When the slave trader came back, she found Dilber where she had left her. They then made their way out of the garden together. When she reached the end of a long road lined with big trees, Dilber turned back and took one final, yearning look at the mansion, at the love nest disguised underneath the feathery morning mist. The mansion that had become her home for years, her sacred shrine of love in the last few months, now stood by itself, between the trees and under the misty sky, in utter silence.

Dilber sat on a rock by the roadside. She wanted to vanish there and then, looking at the house that she was forced to leave forever, her temple of love, as her heart was flooded with many feelings, her profound grief, her abrupt separation from Celal Bey, the heartless humiliations she endured, all of it overwhelmed her. But the slave trader did not allow for any more waiting. As they passed through the gates, Dilber felt a sharp stab in her heart, as if she were taking her last breath.

Down in the village, a few peasants were already on their way to the fields. One could hear the sheep and lambs bleating, and the shepherd herding his flock to the green pastures. The muezzin on the minaret was reciting the call to prayer in the Arab tradition, like they do in Egypt, Algeria and Tunisia.[1] The sound of the prayer reverberated from that spotless marble column all the way to the dark-blue abyss. After it echoed in the clear sky in the tranquil moments of the early morning, it settled back down on earth. The slave trader and Dilber walked on. Suddenly, in the distance there appeared the lonely grave that Celal Bey had shown Dilber only two days ago. They arrived near the grave. The pale rays of the early morning sun seeping through the fence illuminated the tomb. Dilber had remained utterly composed until then, but she felt faint at the sight of the grave. Her face had turned so pale with grief that even the most indifferent of doctors would have been troubled at this sight. She covered her face with her angel-like hands and collapsed at the foot of the grave.

Then this beautiful young woman threw herself on the grave and started sobbing like a five-year-old girl. What unimaginable despair! What inconceivable heartache! Even the yonder peasant paused in the middle of the road upon hearing her sobs. Now the barbaric slave trader panicked, thinking something had happened to the slave girl. She called out to the peasant in the distance for help. ‘Quick, son, fetch some water!’ she said frantically.

[1] The call to prayer (*adhan* in Arabic, *ezan* in Turkish) described here is delivered in a simple, recitative style, typical of rural areas, like the village through which Dilber and the slave trader pass. This contrasts with the ‘*sultani*’ style, which is unique to Istanbul and characterised by its complexity and embellishment, historically performed by muezzins serving in the palaces of the Ottoman sultans.

Chapter 11

That night, after dinner, the family members all gathered in a room. One of Asaf Pasha's nieces was at the piano, playing the end of the garden scene from the famous *Faust* opera, and she looked consumed by every beautiful note. Celal Bey was sitting on a bench next to the piano. He was carried away and subdued by the heavenly harmony arising from those graceful fingers on the piano. His contemplative mood seemed to amuse the young ladies in the room, who were watching his every move from afar.

It may well be true that, after poetry, music offers the greatest comfort to the soul in times of suffering and trepidation, serving as the most beautiful language that the soul can truly hear. As soon as the music stopped, the young ladies, in their youthful exuberance, pulled Celal Bey by the arm and asked with a mischievous smile: 'We haven't seen a new painting from you for a while now. Why is that?'

'I don't know either. I cannot seem to work on any paintings lately'.

Upon hearing this, Miss İclal flashed him one of her charming smiles, ever dangerous for sensitive hearts: 'I guess you are more besotted with a living model rather than interested in painting one'.

The room was filled with laughter at İclal's remarks, but Celal Bey remained silent. As the night went on, these young ladies, like most young girls in our time and age, jumped from one topic to another and finally dwelled on a matter of special interest to them: Miss Tesliye's wedding.

Like all women who loved fashion, the girls first asked about Tesliye's modiste, the colour of her dress and its style. But this lively conversation was interrupted when their father, Münevver Bey, entered the room. All of a sudden, everyone fell silent. To break this awkward silence, Münevver Bey asked Celal Bey whether his sister, Miss Tesliye, who for the time being seemed to be the main topic of conversation in the family, was content with this arranged marriage. Then he told Celal Bey that he, too, hoped that his daughters would soon marry into a noble family.

Lately, Celal Bey had been suffocated by the notion of nobility – his family's sole purpose and fundamental expectation for marriage. To him, nobility was nothing but a ruinous force that had shattered his passionate dreams about happiness and love. The thought that his beloved did not come from a noble family pained him deeply, crushing all his hopes for a union.

'I find the pursuit of nobility to be quite pointless in marriage', said Celal Bey.

His uncle was caught off guard. 'How so?' he asked.

'After all', Celal Bey said, 'isn't it true that a beautiful glance or a sweet smile has enough power to change the mind of even the staunchest advocates of nobility?'

Münevver Bey had been raised with Islamic ethics and was sceptical of the modern sciences, which he thought poisoned young minds with harmful deductions and materialist methods. He was also critical of the spirit of the age, accusing it of stripping young people of their opportunity for any kind of spirituality with endless theories, leading to an absolute lack of faith. He viewed all this with a pessimistic and pious gaze. Thus, he raised his eyebrows and said rather coldly: 'No! Everyone should marry their equal'.

By then, the young girls had already stepped outside, leaving Celal Bey in the room alone with his uncle. After a few minutes of silence, Celal Bey started talking again: 'So you think marriages that are arranged solely for the sake of personal benefits and wealth are morally acceptable?' he asked his uncle.

'Young people should leave the arrangement of their marriages to their parents'.

'I would say that the most important freedom that young people have in this world is to marry whomever they desire. After all, is it not the greatest injustice in the world to interfere with one's freedom to choose a partner, the heart's liberty to decide and the soul's natural inclination to be attracted?'

'Perhaps', his uncle responded, 'but young people are consumed by youthful exuberance, are blinded to the truth, and they are often misguided by their desires. Although youthful fever burns deep, its flames are short-lived. What is left when the whims of youth subside over time? Nothing but mistakes, flaws and perhaps grave wrong-doings'.

'No, no! Uncle, you are not suggesting that young people should approach marriage as if it is a mathematical equation, are you? They always advise young people who are about to get married to remain calm and to make decisions with reason; but as years pass and that calm finally arrives, what then? I cannot imagine anything more meaningless and duller than such a marriage in the first place'.

'All this talk is...' Münevver Bey tried to respond but was interrupted. Celal Bey was thinking about poor Dilber. The thought of her made him even more sentimental, and he continued passionately:

'For a beautiful young girl, to possess a pure heart filled with love, to yearn for affection and to become a source of joy for youthful dreams that picture her amid flowers like a living tableau – this is the greatest privilege and the most natural right that life has granted her. If everyone were to marry when that calm arrived, how could that beautiful girl ever claim her natural right?'

'These words are nothing but the chatter of a mind fired by youthful zeal'.

'No, you're wrong. Without the excitement of the soul and passion, I can neither find purpose in life nor get any pleasure out of it. When one's heart is quieted, they might as well bury him alive'.

Thus far, Celal's uncle had only continued with the conversation to try and change his nephew's mind on the subject. However, realising that his efforts were in vain, he ended the conversation with a disparaging and sardonic smile.

'I am afraid your wife will be the daughter of a farmer', he said.

Celal Bey remained seated for a while. He was lost in thought. Suddenly, he stood up and exclaimed: 'My dear uncle!'

Münevver Bey was taken back by this unexpected childish address of his nephew who had so far been arguing with such fervour yet composure.

'What is it?' he responded with a hint of surprise.

'Would you like to save my life?'

Münevver Bey's astonishment now carried a touch of horror. He asked:

'What are you talking about, my child?'

'I have feelings for someone'.

'For whom?'

'A slave girl'.

'How do you mean, a slave girl?'

'Dilber'.

For a couple of minutes neither of them uttered a word.

'Talk to my father! As you know, my mother worships nobility'.

'This is childish'.

'So be it. When it comes to love, the heart is always a child'.

'Fine, I'll talk to him. But I don't think he'll consent'.

'Still, please talk to him. I don't suppose he'd deny your wishes or break my heart'.

Their conversation had left his uncle deeply conflicted and troubled. Celal kissed his uncle's hand, bid farewell to him and his cousins, then boarded the ferry to return home. On the ferry, he could not help but think what would have happened if his beloved had not been an unfortunate slave. He would in fact fiercely safeguard his decision against all cruel intrusions and defend his right to marry, a right he considered to be entirely his own. But he couldn't do it, and that left him in deep anguish.

These thoughts had even inspired Celal Bey to paint a tableau exposing the unfairness and cruelty of arranged marriages, which served only to deny the desires of the young and secure the approval of their parents. For this painting, he envisioned a bridal chamber to capture the spiritual torment of a young woman married off for wealth and nobility. In a corner of this opulently adorned chamber, the young bride's anguish would be visible in her beautiful gaze and in the delicate lines around her eyes. He planned to depict her disdain for the groom upon seeing him for the first time on their wedding night. He would paint her contempt with the slight downturn of her lips, her clenched teeth visible through her slightly parted lips and her crossed arms. If only he could succeed in capturing, through the right play of colours and lines, the wistful beauty of the bride and the helpless, quiet gaze of her husband, he would display the painting in a museum for all to see. It would stand as a powerful testament, a clear victory over the ideas and conventions unworthy of human dignity and, above all, over those who stood in opposition to his own understanding of love and desire.[1]

[1] The Ottoman literature of the nineteenth century, dating back to works such as İbrahim Şinasi's 1859 play *The Poet's Wedding*, exhibited a long-standing preoccupation with the negative aspects of arranged marriages, subjecting the practice to severe criticism. For Ottoman writers, arranged marriages, much like slavery, were entwined with the prevalent notions of liberty and modernisation that permeated the political discourse.

Chapter 12

When he arrived at the mansion, Celal Bey first greeted his parents and then retired upstairs to his room to work. He had found his mother's complexion rather pale and her speech and demeanour to be unusually subdued. However, he attributed all of this to her recent illness and to a lingering fatigue – the after-effect of neurasthenia that plagues all women – and therefore quieted his concerns. He went to his drawing room, his sanctuary for art. In this room, by the dark-coloured curtains draping the big windows stood half-busts of master artists with their wise foreheads. The walls were covered with unfinished paintings, and in the middle of the room lay painting supplies, scattered, emanating a faint but somewhat unpleasant scent. For nearly half an hour, he wandered among these paint supplies and art tools, trying to put his imagination on the canvas as he envisioned the most hidden points, the darkest aspects, the most difficult intricacies of his subject-matter.

He wanted this new painting to instil an awakening in people's hearts, no matter how small, yet he was unsure about the best approach. Sometimes, a perplexing thought shied away from the cradle of his imagination, like a coy beloved. At other times, he felt the wings of his lofty ideas take flight, like birds, soaring to the world's summit before diving down to gently touch his imagination. The effect of these spiritual pursuits caused a slight tremor in his body and a few tears trickled down his cheeks. To steady his sensitive soul in this delicate task, he longed to see the face of that Caucasian beauty, the one who brought peace to his heart. Yes, he needed to see her. He longed for his beloved's gaze, which filled his mind with amorous thoughts, and her smile, which sparked a thousand brilliant ideas in his mind. Her smile could shed a heavenly light on the hardest and darkest corners of life.

Look at him working in this drawing room. Of course, he needs solitude to execute his art, for it is in those moments of solitude that one's soul enters a state of trance. And of course, he needs his peace and quiet, for it is in that state of peace and quiet that one can listen to the profound voices of the heart.

Celal Bey had been working for over an hour or so, when he noticed someone at the door. He looked up to see who it was.

'What is it, Çaresaz?' he asked.

'Nothing. I was going to tidy up the room'.

'Not now', he told her. But then Celal Bey noticed the look of terror on Çaresaz's face – the familiar fear and despair that invade the faces of all helpless slaves. With the instinct of an artist, he studied her face curiously, wanting to understand her reaction. He continued working on his painting, retracing small details as he spoke gently, in slow, measured words.

'Where's Dilber? Why hasn't she been up here?'

Çaresaz stared at Celal Bey without saying a word. Her eyes were fixed on him. The tragedy of her partner-in-captivity, her dear friend, had left her devastated.

'Çaresaz, what has happened to you? Why won't you respond? Since when do you treat your masters in this manner?'

'Since those masters started to sell off the poor slaves whom they have raised since they were children'.

Celal Bey stopped painting. He looked stupefied.

'I don't understand', he said to Çaresaz, holding on to his paintbrush and palette. 'What are you talking about? Have you lost your mind?'

'Surely masters do not understand the words of a slave. Dilber, that plaything of yours! Dilber, your amusement! Poor girl. If only she had listened to me. Don't you even fear God? After all you have done, you act as if you know nothing about it, as if everything is normal. Show a little mercy! But what am I even talking about? Mercy from a master!'

The paintbrush and the palette fell from Celal Bey's hands as he struggled to get up from his chair like an invalid.

'Tell me at once! Has something happened to Dilber? Where is Dilber?' He repeated these questions over and over. Çaresaz was taken aback by Celal Bey's unexpected reaction. She stepped back to leave the room. 'Dilber has been sold', she said. Her words hit Celal Bey like a flash of lightning, sudden and violent, sending a wave of terror through his nerves. His teeth clenched. Blood rushed to his brain. His body stiffened, and then he fell to the ground like a statue.

Chapter 13

Celal Bey was consumed by a raging brain fever that tormented him. Zehra Hanım, with all her motherly affection, the kind that constitutes the noblest scene in the entire universe, remained by her son's side throughout the night, holding his hand as he lay unconscious, uncertain of what else she could do. Desperate for an answer, she kept asking: 'Celal, how are you feeling? Tell me, where does it hurt?' Again and again, but to no avail. She received no response from Celal Bey.

Celal Bey's fever had subsided with the arrival of the blessed morning. Zehra Hanım, waiting by her ailing son's bed, noticed that he was about to gain consciousness, so she leaned over him and asked: 'My Celal, my dear! How are you?' Celal's lips moved. And when she leaned closer and listened to him, she could hear him whisper the name 'Dilber'. Oh, that terrifying name! A name that would shatter her son's future and ruin the fortune of her house! Zehra Hanım looked as if haunted by a dreadful vision and slowly walked out the door.

When she returned to her room, Asaf Pasha asked after his son. Knowing that she would tear up if she were to speak, Zehra Hanım remained silent for a while. And when words finally came out of her lips, she was in tears.

'Oh, I have committed such a crime. I've ruined my son's life with my own hands. He was consumed by fever all night, and the first thing that came out of his mouth when he opened his eyes was "Dilber". Oh, I cannot bear it'.

After a moment of contemplation, Asaf Pasha lit his cigarette. 'Do not let one night's fever shatter your determination', he told his wife. 'I will not yield to this madness, the whims of a young heart'.

But Zehra Hanım had witnessed how her beloved son had fallen into the hands of brain fever. A motherly affection dawned on her like a revelation, and suddenly she let go of all her desires and convictions.

'No, no. I will have Dilber brought back right away', she said to her husband. 'I thought it was just a fleeting fancy. But it isn't, and I cannot make my child martyr for an idea, for a stubborn resolve. What use is fortune to me if he is gone?'

This time, Asaf Pasha responded firmly. 'Ah, mothers!' he said. 'They are always the ones to ruin their children's future. Believe me, it's just another small whim, a fleeting fancy, a passing desire. His suffering was just for one night, and it has already passed. That's all. You want to start all over again. Do what you must do, but don't expect me to give my consent'.

In the meantime, Celal Bey had gotten out of his bed and was pacing the room. Once in a while, the terrible trauma and shock that he had endured sent shivers through his body. In those moments, he felt pulled into the depths of a chasm opening in front of him, making him dizzy. Was he sick? No, not really! He could feel the core of his existence being shaken by this agony, as if the very means of survival, power, strength, courage had all abandoned him to the hands of a nothingness that looked more terrifying than death. In his weary state, he collapsed on a nearby chair and fixed his gaze on a single point. His mind, like a lamp illuminating a dark grave, filled with sorrowful thoughts and lost hopes. A deep urge to cry, like a child, welled up within him, but he could not cry. He stayed like this for a few hours. As it so often happens in moments of hardship, a sudden shift took hold. The savage force that had plunged him into sorrow and suffering appeared before his eyes with its vile face. Overcome by frenzy, he sprang to his feet and began pacing the room like a restless lion trapped in a cage.

As Celal Bey paced the room, haunted by these ghastly thoughts, he was muttering to himself: 'Dilber! Who knows whose slave she is now!' And when all hopes, dreams and strength abandoned him, he abruptly stopped, standing there motionless. He gazed far into the distance, his eyes lost in the void ahead.

How vulnerable and weak was Celal Bey in this moment. His nerves were ailing, and his mind, plagued with desperation, was unable to ward off the many horrific ideas that crossed it. Hopeless, miserable and sad, he leaned against the window and watched the white clouds floating around like soap bubbles before they disappeared in the north wind. He suddenly felt the urge to get some fresh air, hoping it would ease the laboured breathing that had been troubling him since yesterday. He got dressed, grabbed his walking stick and left the house without saying a word to anyone. He turned his back to the garden, a place filled with a thousand cherished memories of love, and then slowly continued his way without casting even a single glance back. Nature went on in its harmony and joy, utterly indifferent to his sorrow, while his haunted gaze swept over its ornaments with a sullen face.

He walked on until he saw the small grave on the hill. Moved by this sight, he decided to veer from his path and walk up the hill. When he reached the top, he rested under a tree. His eyes, heavy with weariness and exhaustion, lingered for minutes wherever they fell before finally turning toward the waters of the Sea of Marmara. Falcons and swallows were flying towards the lovelorn dusk, singing an inspiring love song. Meanwhile, a steamboat slowly sailed toward the horizon, its smoke trailing like a thin black line against the sky, slicing through the sun as it sank into the water, like a fiery orb. Celal called out to the ship, with a scream coming from the deepest corner of his heart: 'Dilber, Dilber!'

At that moment, a faint sound carried by a gentle breeze reached his ear. He turned, listening intently. In times of despair and distress, doesn't everyone await solace, even from the blowing wind and drifting clouds? And so did Celal Bey yearn for signs from the faintest sounds and movements. Alas, there was nothing other than despair. The voice got closer. It belonged to a peasant who worked in the fields. His mind was unburdened by any thoughts of the future, and his needs in life were simple. He walked with an easy, carefree joy, singing as he faced the setting sun:

Ah my little one, my dear,
How I long to see you near,
I vow, I sigh,
For you I'd die right here.
Are you tired walking up the hill?
Did my words make your heart chill?
Since you became my lover,
You are to embrace me, still.

Oh, blessed man! Blessed man! How deeply Celal envied and admired the happiness of this man, untouched by society's pathetic calculations and comparisons, freed from its superstitions and customs that turned its members into captives. The modern sciences, the pinnacle of human understanding, and the experiential philosophy of Schopenhauer – along with the influence of science, which meticulously dissects matter and nature, only to offer pessimistic and bleak conclusions – had, wherever they took hold, destroyed all the lofty aspirations that sustain life and stripped humanity of its consolations. They turned thoughts into the despairing cries of owls among ruins and, in their spiritual effect, poisoned both the minds and bodies of the young. Celal Bey longed, if only for a moment, to share in the happiness of this man, whose mind was free of such intellectual catastrophes.

'Look here! Where are you going?' he called out to him.

The peasant stopped singing and said: 'What do you want?'

Celal Bey walked towards him slowly. He did not really know how to start a conversation with him, but then he handed the peasant a cigarette and asked: 'Do you have a match? Let's have a cigarette'.

'Yes, I do', the peasant said, putting down the sack filled with his daily harvest, his treasure and pride. He pulled a match from his sash, and they each lit a cigarette.

'What is inside this sack?' Celal Bey asked.

'That's my daily bread', the peasant answered. He pointed to a field more than half ploughed and said: 'I work there during the day. I put in this sack whatever God has given me that day and take it to my home. My wife and I, we say our graces, pray for our Sultan, and eat our daily bread'.

'So you're married?' Celal Bey asked. 'Have you been married for a long time?'

'It's been two months since I took my betrothed as my wife. She's waiting for me at home now. My feet dance back home to reunite with her every night. But tell me, did you not attend our wedding in the village?'

'No, I haven't', Celal Bey said. 'Is your wife beautiful?'

A sour expression crossed the peasant's face. 'That's none of your business. Don't ask such private questions', he said.

Celal Bey, realising he had made a mistake, said: 'Sorry, I misspoke, I meant to ask are you happy?'

'Why wouldn't I be happy?' the peasant responded. 'I have every reason to be grateful for what I have. When I look at the wealthy and genteel folks, I can't help but feel grateful for having just enough to eat. Just three days ago, I saw an elegant lady, on the other side of this field, by the grave on the hilltop. She was on her knees, sobbing'.

Celal Bey suddenly stood up and then quickly sat down again.

The peasant kept talking: 'It seems that even the hearts underneath those fancy clothes cannot find much peace. I looked at her, and my heart ached. There was an elderly woman with her. She asked me to bring water for the young lady. Wait, are you crying? Why would anyone start crying for no reason?'

'No, I am not crying. Keep talking. Tell me the whole story, quickly', said Celal Bey.

The peasant continued: 'After a while, I got it. Slave! She was a slave! I reckoned she's done something wrong, her mistress got upset and put her up for sale. You know better, but it's not right to make those poor slaves cry'.

He looked at Celal Bey and with the carefree attitude of peasants asked: 'Is something bothering you? You've gone as pale as a ghost'.

'No', Celal Bey said. 'I'm telling you, it's nothing; keep going. Tell me. What did you do then? What happened to that girl? Where did she go?'

'Nothing happened!' the peasant explained. 'We gave the poor girl some water to drink and sprinkled some on her face. Then, the elderly woman held her by the hand, and they went on their way. You are really weeping like a child! If something is bothering you, leave it in God's hands. Whatever he decides for you, it will be good'.

'Do you know where that girl went?' Celal Bey asked.

'No. They headed towards the pier, and I went back to the field'.

'If you let me know where she went, I will give you a hundred liras', Celal Bey insisted.

The peasant took a step back as if he were scared and said: 'One-hundred liras! The girl! I swear, I don't know. You should have told me about this before. But how would you know? One-hundred liras! The girl! One-hundred liras! The girl!' After thinking about it for a moment, he put his sack on his back and said: 'I know not where she is, nor can I find her. Farewell, may Allah keep you safe'.

As he walked away, he was back to singing his song:

The boxwood won't shed its leaves
True love never from the heart flees
Once I have set my eyes on you, my love
No one else would please.

As the peasant's song started to fade away in the distance, Celal Bey was overtaken by a strong urge to cry, but he couldn't. Instead, he felt his soul drown in his tears. He cried out Dilber's name in anguish one last time, towards the hills and meadows of Çamlıca.[1] Then he headed back home. But alas, his legs, too weak to carry the weight of his burden, forced him to kneel in the middle of the road ever so often.

When he finally arrived home and heard his mother's anxious voice calling out 'Celal! Where have you been?' he collapsed into her arms and started to sob like a child. In his mother's compassionate embrace, his sole refuge from his sorrows in this world, his tears flowed like a

[1] A district on the Asian shore of Istanbul, popular for its hills and public parks offering panoramic views of the Sea of Marmara in the nineteenth century. Like many wealthy Ottoman families, Sezai's family owned a summer mansion in Çamlıca. It was there that Sezai met Abdülhak Hamit Tarhan (1852–1937) and Recaizade Mahmut Ekrem (1847–1914), two of the most significant writers of the late-nineteenth-century new literature movement, who would become his lifelong friends.

river, drowning his very soul and putting out the spark of life within him, eventually finding their way into his mother's heart.

No matter what stage of life one may be in, a person is always a child in the eyes of their mother. Truly, nothing in the world can awaken a woman's compassion more deeply than the tears of an honourable man, especially when that woman is a mother.

Chapter 14

He was knocking on the door! He was knocking impatiently, like a sinner from Hell seeking refuge at the gates of Heaven. He occasionally pleaded in desperation: 'Open the door!'

Celal Bey was on a street with an elderly woman by his side. In front of him was a run-down bakery, with its ancient shutters firmly closed. Above the bakery was a dilapidated house on the brink of collapse, its colourful top windows broken. It looked as though a Janissary might peer out from behind them. Two swallows nested inside the house, darting in through the doors and out the windows. Right next to this house was an abandoned smithy, and at the end of the street was another road. Celal Bey stood under a relentless rain that could melt away all patience and endurance; he stubbornly knocked at the door of this house, yet no one answered.

But Celal Bey could no longer stand the silence. Overtaken by a sudden fit of madness, he battered down the already dilapidated door with a few forceful punches and stormed into the house.

Moments later, he had dragged a man whom he had found asleep in the house out into the street by his collar. He started yelling: 'Tell me! Where is Dilber? If you don't tell me where she is, if you hide anything from me, I swear by Allah that I will bury you alive right now!' In that delirium, Celal Bey had grabbed the man's shirt so forcefully that it tore to pieces, and yet Celal Bey was still attacking him and asking repeatedly: 'Aren't you going to tell me?' Poor guy, he didn't know why he had this grip of fate on his collar. He kept saying: 'What do you want from me? What did I do to you?'

The raucous noise on the street had reached the neighbourhood watchman. He emerged from around the corner, stretching his arms languidly, seemingly woken up from his nap.

'What's all this?' he inquired, but his speech got interrupted by his ceaseless yawning. 'What's the problem between you two?' he asked the two men. The elderly woman, standing behind Celal Bey, stepped forward and asked the watchman in a shaky voice: 'My son, where did the people in the house go?'

'They moved out the other day. They left the city, but for where, I don't know,' he replied to the woman. Then he turned to Celal Bey: 'What is it that you want from this poor fellow?' he asked. Celal Bey let go of the man, and after standing there for a while, petrified, he said to the watchman: 'If you tell me where they went, I will reward you'. The watchman, after considering the offer, replied: 'You tell me where you live. I'll ask around. I'll eventually hear something for sure, and then I'll bring the news to you. The owner was an elderly lady...' He started to recount the events but was interrupted by the slave trader woman who had sold Dilber to this household: 'I didn't know these people either. That night, in a rush, they told me about this house. Ah, I wish I at least remembered their names...'

Before she could finish her sentence, Celal Bey threateningly walked towards her and yelled: 'You, human trader! You, the traitor of the kingdom of humanity! Go to hell! If you weren't a woman, I would have strangled you with my own hands'. She glanced around a few times, terrified, and then quickly disappeared in the streets. As for Celal Bey, after he had paid for the door that he had broken down, the neighbourhood watchman let him go.

What to do now? Should one endure life, engulfed in an infernal fire, until the end? When your life's purpose is gone, what joy remains there in living?

It was raining! It was raining! It was pouring relentlessly. The beautiful body that he had painted many times, the body that had allowed him to discover the endless joys of his noble art, where was she? What vile savage's arms were she to fall into now?

And even if he could forget it all, how could he forget those sparkling eyes, like the reflection of dawn on a mirror, the gates to her soul! Losing Dilber's smile would mean losing the joy of his mornings; not seeing her eyes would mean losing the twin stars that guided his fate. How could he ever again find any beauty or pleasure in the morning sun or the stars? Without her, the sky, the earth and the entire universe seemed empty, meaningless and dark. Now that he was cast out of that world of beauty, torn from its realm, from the air she breathed, he no longer saw a reason to go on living. He had been deprived not only of her, but of his very muse. For who would whisper to him the boundless secrets of love once inspired by those eyes now? How was he to grasp the meaning of eternity hidden within that smile? Where else could he ever come across such a face, with its perfect complexion and features, which he regarded as the most spectacular masterpiece in the book of beauty? When Celal considered all this, he found life without Dilber utterly meaningless.

It was raining! It was raining! It was pouring relentlessly.

He passed by the houses but did not feel the rain streaming from the eaves, trickling down his collar onto his body, nor did he notice the mud rising to his knees as he walked on. Where is Dilber now, he wondered. In Asia? In Africa? Had Celal been a medieval king, he would have declared war on Asia, that savage old tyrant raised on blood, and on Africa, where a mere lizard becomes a crocodile and a cat turns into a tiger. Hopeless and weary, he walked on, repeating to himself aloud: 'Oh! I'm in such agony!'

Suicide, people's way of resigning from the duties and commands of creation, a disturbed mind's weapon of enmity against destiny, the armed daughter of sorrow, was now whispering rather timidly, rather slowly into Celal's ears: 'I can save you from this eternal agony!' Feeling his body tremble from head to toe, he quickened his pace and stepped onto the ferry. He was still muttering to himself 'Yes! Yes!' when he settled into a corner of the cabin, where there were two other men, deep in conversation. When one of the two companions noticed Celal Bey, he discreetly gestured at him.

'Look, our friend over there is talking to himself!' he said mockingly.

'Yes! Madness comes in many forms!' his friend said. They both laughed at Celal.

Five minutes later, another man entered the cabin with a newspaper in his hand. When he saw Celal Bey, he eagerly approached him and shook his hand. They started to talk about this and that.

'How are you?' Celal Bey asked.

'I am well. How are you?' the man responded.

'Thanks be to God', Celal Bey said.

'I saw you on the way here, you were walking very fast'.

'I didn't want to miss the ferry', Celal Bey explained.

The two men in the corner, who had been listening in, couldn't help but laugh at Celal Bey's final words. They were the kind with no intellectual pursuits – idlers who spent their time eavesdropping on conversations in the streets and on ferries, chiming in uninvited and ridiculing everything around them.

'I think you are mistaken', Celal Bey's friend said. 'There's still about twenty minutes until the departure of the ferry'.

'Yes', he said. 'My watch has been deceiving me for the past few days. I say it's deceiving, but it's almost mocking me. At times, it rushes me to the point of exhaustion, and at other times it allows for such long pauses that I miss the ferry. A faulty watch is like a mind with impaired judgment'.

'It's been a while since we last saw each other. I haven't run into you anywhere. You seem a bit pale today. I hope you are not unwell', his friend remarked.

'No', Celal Bey said. 'I'm fine. It's been quite rainy; I think I've caught a cold'.

Even after five or ten minutes, Celal Bey was yet to turn a single page of the book he appeared to be reading. This detail amused the two men in the corner, men who envied every virtue that they lacked and took petty revenge on anything noble, with their crude, thoughtless mockery. Whispering to each other, they exchanged sly remarks and broke into fits of quiet laughter.

But Celal was in a miserable state. His mind and body were in turmoil. His fierce anger would sometimes be followed by an eerie, almost death-like coldness and calm, and at other times his unsettling stillness would suddenly erupt into a storm of fury. And that's exactly what happened in that moment. Celal sprang to his feet and with a Herculean grip grabbed one of the men laughing at him by the collar. First, he yanked him upright and then forcefully pushed him down on the floor.

He said: 'You've been staring at me and laughing all this time. Now, try crying under my feet for a change. If you don't tell me the reason why you were laughing, I will crush you under my feet. Tell me what you know that I don't! Tell me! Or… or are you some sort of a slave trader?'

Men like these – vulgar and boundlessly insolent – always cower in fear when the very dignity and honour that they trample at every turn rise up with newfound strength to confront them. The man whom Celal Bey grasped in his mighty grip begged desperately for mercy, while his friend, seized with panic, tried to slip out through the door that Celal Bey was blocking. But Celal Bey grabbed him by the arm as well and demanded: 'Why did you keep staring and laughing at me like that? Or is she… is she at your house? Do you do slave trading for a living? Tell me! If you're hiding the truth from me, there's no escape for either of you!'

Celal Bey's friend was shocked by the unexpected terror that seemed to have seized his friend. He dropped his newspaper and stepped between them. He pleaded with Celal Bey, trying to calm him down. 'Don't mind them!' he said to his friend. 'And besides, does fighting in the cabins suit someone like you? Have a seat, please. I believe you will agree with me that you need to protect your dignity'. Celal Bey sank back to his seat as he slowly regained his composure. Then, as he struggled to catch his breath, he turned to his friend and said: 'I beg you! Tell me if she's with you! I'll pay however many thousands of liras you want. I'll pay it!' But later, when he fully came to his senses, he said, as if waking from a dream: 'What was I saying? Their demeaning attitude suddenly struck a nerve in me... Please forgive me, I didn't mean to cause you trouble'.

The ferry was docking at Kadıköy Pier, and as soon as it did, the two men beaten by Celal hurried out of the cabin.

It was raining! It was raining! It was pouring relentlessly.

On his way home, Celal Bey saw an elderly woman and a young girl walk past him and turn into a side street. Like a hawk spotting a prey, he raised his head, fixed his gaze in their direction and said; 'That's her... right there!' Without hesitation, Celal Bey turned into the street and began following the elderly woman and the young girl. The way in which the girl walked and swayed... Especially that captivating figure... It's her... It has to be her, he told himself... The way she held her umbrella, the way she walked beside the elderly woman in silence, pensive, carrying that sorrowful air around her... There was no doubt in his mind. It was her.

But a violent palpitation shattered his stride, and something took away his strength to follow them. See, Celal Bey had such respect for women – or, in other words, for the honour of his nation – that, even in his moment of madness, he still couldn't bring himself to cry out to them in the middle of the street, asking them to stop and wait for him. The urge burned strong, yet he held back. The truth he was about to discover filled him with such dread that he couldn't bring himself to approach them. He couldn't bear the sadness if it wasn't Dilber, nor the overwhelming joy if it was her. He thought to himself: 'Ah, if only I could find her, nothing in the entire world could ever tear her away from me!'

The two women headed towards the door of a big house... They were about to disappear into the house. Just once, just one glimpse! But it was impossible! His legs were shaking, and he was out of breath. Just as the women reached the door and were about to step inside, Celal Bey, like a flash of lightning, rushed past them and leaned on a wall in an attempt to see their faces. But alas, this young girl... She wasn't Dilber.

Chapter 15

Celal had spent the entire week in unspeakable agony. In those unending days of madness, he developed a habit of wandering on the streets. He would attack anyone who stared at him for too long and even people who passed by him silently like spectres, clad in the mysterious cloak of darkness, appearing and disappearing in the longest night of longing. He would shout at them: 'You have her… She is in your house… If you give her to me, I'll give you anything you want. If you hide her from me, I'll kill you!'

Once, on a secluded street, he even accosted a young man simply because he seemed to be enjoying life, because his face radiated like a freshly bloomed flower and his laughter sounded effortless as he chatted with his friends. While Celal himself was crushed under the unbearable burden of life, this man seemed to move through it with ease. Consumed with bitterness, Celal lashed out at him. 'Why are you so happy?' he confronted the young man, shouting: 'That only means that she… You definitely have her… Now, one of us will face his fate!'

This young man wanted to hand Celal to the police, but a wise friend stopped him. 'Let the poor soul go', he said. As they walked a little further away, he added: 'Believe it or not, this unfortunate man was once among the most talented artists. I suppose he must have become a shadow of his old self after he suffered the loss of his beloved. You can hear it maybe not so much in what he said, but certainly in how he said it'.

One morning that same week, Celal Bey was returning from the Fener Lighthouse which resembled a green raft floating on the clear waters of the Sea of Marmara.[1] As the morning light spread across the sky, it seemed to

[1] Fener, also known as Fener Garden (or by its modern name, Fenerbahçe), refers to a peninsula on the Asian side near Moda, named after the lighthouse ('fener') constructed in 1562, where Asaf Pasha built his mansion.

Figure 16 Lighthouse at Fener. Courtesy of IBB Atatürk Library.

turn transparent. He breathed freely beneath this clear canopy and walked along a tranquil path through the countryside. Sometimes, he would lie down on the green grass, gazing up at the sky, and ask in a whisper: 'My God, what should I do?'

He walked in the silence of the countryside for a while. As he passed by Moda Point, he heard people crying inside a house. He suddenly stopped. 'There's crying in this house… That means Dilber is here…' he said to himself. Without hesitation, Celal walked up and knocked on the door and asked the elderly woman who opened the door: 'Who is crying upstairs?' The woman mistook him for one of the regular guests of this household and replied: 'Ah, haven't you heard? The Efendi of the house has passed away'. Celal Bey turned to the other guests who were there for the funeral. 'Forget about this poor soul!' he said, 'I am the one who truly died. Bury me instead'.

Chapter 16

Celal Bey had never been so distraught before. For three days, he spoke not a single word to anyone in the house. On the third night, he paced all night on the balcony where he had first seen Dilber. From time to time, he gazed onto the horizon, as if he were waiting for someone. Each time the breeze came rushing from the sea, tossing Celal's unkempt hair across his face, it unsettled his nerves more, and in those moments he stood still and listened to the sound of the waves crashing on the shore.

The eastern sky was still dim, and the western sky was completely swallowed in darkness. Beneath him, the sea, whipped into a frenzy by the intensifying wind, howled in agony. Restless, Celal stood there, waiting for the arrival of the morning, as if it carried a promise for his fading hope.

A little later, he collapsed into a nearby armchair. As the morning broke, illuminating the East with its grandeur and majesty, he fixed his half-open eyes on a distant point and suddenly began to scream: 'I found it! I found it!' What was it that he saw in front of his eyes? Was it a spectre flashing before his eyes, or was it one of those creatures that his sickly mind offered his suspicious eyes? Whatever it was, he sprang to his feet, like Archimedes did after his *eureka* moment, and started running through the house bare-headed and barefoot, screaming: 'I found it!' In that frenzy, he roused everyone in the house, until they stopped him at the main gate, right before he tried to go out into the street. Suddenly, it seemed like the vision in front of his eyes had entirely vanished. He went upstairs to the room where his mother, father and sister were. He was in a trance. He looked at everyone but recognized no one.

'Celal! Have mercy on your mother', his mother cried, but Celal stood there numb, unmoved. After a moment, he slowly moved toward his sister and paused. Then, forcing the words from his lips, he said: 'She is now… an odalisque!' He then clasped his hands tightly and suddenly collapsed into his sister's arms, unconscious. As they carried him to his bed, both his mother and sister were in tears. That very morning, the doctors examined him and, after talking amongst themselves, concluded that he was suffering from a serious case of brain fever. Although he was in critical condition, they assured the family that it wasn't an entirely hopeless case.

Chapter 17

In Egypt, a merchant, who had accumulated unimaginable wealth thanks to the twists of fate and the times in which he lived, had built a house after the Alhambra Palace.[1] This house had all the captivating and enchanting grandeur of the supreme Arabic architecture that surpasses and dwarfs even the highest degree of fine arts with its ornate details, fine embellishments and sublime essence.

At the entrance was a grand salon. At its centre, a low ebony settee adorned with delicate floral engravings commanded attention, while columns of red imperial marble, a hallmark of Arabic architecture, rose in the corners.[2] The walls were embellished with gold leaf against a backdrop of red and turquoise, and the crown mouldings were decorated with verses praising the beauty of African gardens and the Nile. That night, this grand salon was filled with singers and dancers, bringing a tale from *A Thousand and One Nights* to life.

The windows of this chamber opened onto vast and delightful gardens, from which pleasant scents wafted inside, carried by a soft breeze, like

[1] Famous Islamic palace in Granada, Andalusia, Spain, its core dating to the thirteenth century. The American writer Washington Irving's *Tales of the Alhambra*, published in 1832, introduced the palace to the western world as an exotic place. But it was after Owen Jones's groundbreaking publication *Plans, Elevations, Sections and Details of the Alhambra*, published in London between 1842 and 1845, that an architectural style called 'Alhambresque' became widely popular, first in Europe and then in the Ottoman Empire, known as Ottoman Orientalism or Renaissance. Sezai is referencing this trend in architecture when he is writing about the mansion in Egypt.

[2] Porphyry, known as 'imperial marble', is an igneous rock similar to granite but featuring large, light-coloured crystals embedded in a fine-grained red or purple matrix. The term 'porphyry' originates from the Latin word for purple, the colour of Roman nobility. This prestigious stone, used exclusively by Imperial Rome for various ornamental objects, was sourced from Egypt.

Figure 17 Palm forest by the Nile. Courtesy of IBB Atatürk Library.

the breath of a mysterious fairy. The scents emanated from orange tree blossoms and wove through wide banana leaves that draped over the high garden walls, creating the illusion of a lush green curtain embracing the garden. As the gaze wandered toward the far end of the garden, one could see the pyramids, which had endured the blows of nature for thousands of years and still seemed resolute in preventing the destructive deluge of time. From behind the pyramids, from the towering date palms whose drooping leaves echoed the sorrow of the desert and stirred the heart, and from the pond that wore the reflections of the far-reaching rays of the African dusk, casting everything in a rosy hue, there came a gentle, pleasant breeze on this calm night.

A scene from a fairy tale! Dazzling Circassian girls, dressed in white atlas silk, sat beneath the towering columns, their long hair falling on the cushions. They played violins, kanuns, ouds, singing a heavenly tune that could summon the angels from the skies. Dancing before the musicians were twenty or twenty-five unrivalled beauties. They wore gilded, light-blue velvet *saltamarka*s, their wavy hair falling to their knees, their décolletés revealing their pure white bosoms that forever arrested anyone who worshipped beauty.[3]

[3] A Greek word used for short jackets for women.

As the girls danced and played their music, the merchant reclined on the ebony settee, utterly intoxicated by the blissful atmosphere. The soul-soothing harmony arising from the beauty and flowers around him seemed to lull his very soul.

In this exuberant gathering of the Orient, which, like its fairy tales, had captivated all of Europe and glamorised every fantasy, the most striking sight was the gaze and smile of an oud-playing girl among the musicians. From time to time, her sorrowful gaze escaped through her long lashes, which cast a shadow on her silky, transparent skin. Like the morning star diffusing its faint beams through the leaves, her eyes passed the open windows and drifted toward the garden. In those moments, while everyone around her appeared cheerful, joyous and exalted, a melancholic smile lingered on her half-open, pale lips, like white butterflies whirling around the petal of an autumn rose, silently bearing witness to the anguish of a tender heart.

From afar, the girl's grace and beauty set her apart from the dazzling women around her. Yet her head kept sinking forward, as if weighed down by invisible sorrow. Was it the heaviness of her thick, dark hair, which only made her pale skin seem even more delicate? Or the piercing, intoxicating scent of the flowers, made more overpowering by the night's damp air? If one could look even closer, one would hear a name hovering on her lips, as faint as the chirping of baby birds in a nest, followed by a clandestine wail, a sighing 'ah', that trailed after that name.

Out of respect for this young girl's delicate situation and the secret in her young heart, let us not pry any further!

But why is she so sad? Why is she so very tormented?

In a dark corner, hidden behind a majestic column, stood a harem eunuch, one of those fiercely loyal servants who would gladly give their lives for their masters. His fingers were entwined in his thick and curly hair, and he was thinking about something. He had already announced to everyone that his wealthy, powerful master had taken a particular liking to this girl. He had also given the good news directly to the girl herself, as if delivering a blessing.

Our pen respects the guarding of secrets and, therefore, it doesn't allow us to pry any further. After all, aren't the deepest secrets of young girls always betrayed by a tear or a smile?

When joy and cheer had overtaken the room, the chief eunuch – let us call him by his name, Cevher – looked pensive. Who knows what he was really thinking, but judging by his face, as dark as a stormy night, and his eyes, as bright as lightning, one might say that he was perhaps cursing nature for his blackness and the Sudanese for his castration.

Chapter 17

Poor Cevher! He had been captured from a desert; a desert with no waterside to sing by, no trees to climb and cry out about in joy, no greenery to animate nature. They had taken him from the desert and put him, like a clipped bird without wings, in a garden decorated with thousands of colourful flowers, cascades, green trees rising to a dark-blue sky. They had taken him from the Sudanese desert, scorched by the blazing sun, and placed him in the salons of Egypt. Just as a bird in a garden looks longingly at the passing clouds and the trees where other birds freely perch and take flight, so too did Cevher look upon these lustrous salons and heavenly beauties with the same burning desire. And just as that bird longs to soar into the vast sky above, only to realise that its wings were no more, so too did Cevher feel trapped in the hellish fires of deprivation every time he met the endlessly deep, sky-like blue eyes of a beautiful girl.

Cevher's eyes were fixed on the girl playing the oud. She certainly stood out to him. With her rather graceful figure, pure beauty and soul-nourishing sweetness, she was unlike any of the other girls. Yet something about this slave girl unsettled him. The sorrow in her eyes planted a seed of doubt in Cehver's heart. He watched her intently, unable to look away, determined to either disperse his suspicions or uncover the truth.

It was a moonlit African winter night, brighter than any winter day in Europe, especially in London. They were rowing across the shimmering waters of the garden pond. Its waters had remained pure, untouched – like a child – since the dawn of creation and thus was worthy of being called the mirror of love. The water, springing from the pumice stones at the pond's edge, flowed beneath the admiring gaze of the trees, meandering across the lawn. Nourishing the grass and carving little paths, it became a vessel taking the mind back to mythological times. In the stillness of the night, the reflections of the trees rippled and danced on the water, petals of a thousand colours drifting gently down, carried by the current to its beautiful shores. Cevher rowed among boats carrying fair-haired girls, whose locks gleamed under the moonlight like strands of gold. He had taken the slave girl, whom he had not let out of his sight for days, into a small boat and was quietly rowing towards a secluded spot.

When he reached the other side of the pond, he found an acacia tree whose long branches, like a woman's hair, shimmered under the luminescent night sky and danced in the blue waters of the pond. He tied the boat, then turned to the girl, who still seemed lost in melancholy, and said: 'You are pensive. Always pensive! But tell me, who are you thinking of? Don't be afraid of me! Consider me your confidant! Just because my face is dark, does that mean that my soul is, too? My body may be lacking, but don't I still have a heart? Am I not capable of pity or love? Think of me as a friend, a brother, or, if you wish, a sister. Now, let's have a talk heart-to-heart'.

Cevher could see that the girl was moved by his perceptiveness toward her suffering, but she did not have the courage to reveal her heart's deepest secrets. She looked hesitant.

'Don't worry! Nobody can hear us. Don't be afraid! These trees, these flowers, they are all tight-lipped. They're not people, so they won't betray you', Cevher encouraged Dilber.

The slave girl's eyes welled with tears at these words. 'What's the point of me telling you about my secrets, my sorrows? Wouldn't it be cruel to tear your compassionate heart apart with my story?'

Cevher responded with sincere enthusiasm: 'Oh, not at all, not at all. I can save you! I can find a remedy for your troubles. Tell me! Tell me how you were separated from your dear mother. Tell me what you felt, whether it has not been long since you were taken captive, when you placed your head on your beloved's knees by a riverbank and watched the snow-capped mountains of your homeland! Have you ever waited for your lover or fiancée under the towering trees in the depths of vast and wild forests? If you did, how fast did your heart beat? How did the birds chirp in the forest? How anxious was your mother when you came home late? Tell me all of it. Tell me all about it, and I'll tell you how happy I was in my mother's frail arms, shielded from the scorching sun and the fierce desert lions. I'll tell you how the melancholic songs of the girls carrying water jugs on their heads still echo in my ears. Ah, you wouldn't know. I believed that no creature in the world could be more beautiful than those desert fairies. In the blistering heat of the desert, how pleasing those dark faces seemed! Africa, the land that ripens all creatures and all things beyond their bounds and before their time, had also awoken my manhood. Every now and then I'd tell myself that their curly locks clinging to a heart like ivy, tight and gripping, must be so perilous. Ah, what did I know? I imagined even the angels in the heavens as black. And now! Ah, look at me now! Come, if you wish, let's weep over our sad fate together!'

When Cevher had finished his words, the young slave girl was looking down, nervously fiddling with the sleeves of her dress. 'I don't have any troubles', she said. 'But I cannot live here. I need to go to Istanbul'.

'To Istanbul?' Cevher asked. 'Why is that? Why?'

'Because…'

'Ah, I understand! Say it now!'

'Because if I stay here, I cannot live. Because…' All of a sudden, the slave girl broke into tears and started sobbing on Cevher's chest. Cevher wrapped his rather thin and disproportionately long arms around her, embracing this radiant beauty who sought refuge in him. He lifted his grieving eyes to the sky. 'My God!' he said. 'Do you see this poor Dilber?'

On this divine African night, beneath the graceful canopy of a tree by the edge of a heavenly pond, Dilber had found the perfect spot to confess her love. She wept in the arms of Cevher, who had always taken pity on her since the day she arrived, patiently reassuring her that he was both a sister and a friend to her in her times of hardship.

'Enough now', Cevher said. 'You shattered my heart into a thousand pieces, enough!' Then, leaning closer to her ear, he whispered: 'I can save you. For God's sake, enough now'.

As they rowed that small boat back towards the house, Cevher tried to soothe Dilber with reassuring words and promises of salvation. When they reached the edge of the lake, the melodies of the ouds and violins still filled the air. The girls, now making their way back to the mansion, passed through the trees and across the lawn; from a distance, they resembled angelic figures in grand paintings, drifting among clouds or the mist. Cevher and Dilber joined them as they all returned to the mansion.

Cevher had now become like a shadow to that divine beauty, never leaving her side. So closely did he keep watch over her that even the night could not separate them.

Dilber retreated to her bedroom, but even in bed she found no comfort. After a restless night, she rose at twilight. As she stepped out of her room, she was startled by a dark shape on the threshold. She looked carefully at the dark shape. Surprised and saddened by the sight in front of her eyes, she asked: 'Cevher! Why are you sleeping here on the floor?'

From where he lay, Cevher turned to her and said: 'I have been waiting on you here so you could sleep peacefully in your room!'

Chapter 18

Dilber had been through countless trials and tribulations, had shed many tears over her woes and misery and in the end grown to loathe the unceasing injustices of humanity. Yet the innate grace of her peaceful nature had never been rattled by anger. But that morning there was anger in her tearful eyes, directed at the woman pretending to be nice to her. Dilber's words carried a piercing resonance as they fell from her lips, and her entire demeanour was marked by a strange effervescence. There was so much she wanted to say but couldn't. Her heart swelled. She was infuriated. Her beautiful pearly-white teeth chattered, trapping so many words that she longed to say in her mouth. Her voice was silenced by tears; her body surrendered to shivers that conquered the soul in moments of intense awe and hatred. She shuddered at the thought of her love for Celal Bey being trampled on. She refused to hear that ugly proposal, covered her ears to shut it out, yet it was too late. It had already unnerved her, stirring her heart like a storm stirs up a still pond. When the wealthy merchant heard that a purchased slave was refusing him, that she was unmoved by his offers, indifferent to the rare, jewelled treasures that crowned the eastern dreams of India, he resorted to threats and even force. But it was all in vain! Perhaps this slave was a stubborn soul, blind to reason, ungrateful for the graciousness shown to her, or a rebel defiant against her master's command. No! Not so for those who understood the human heart. Dilber had steeled herself with an impenetrable iron will, impervious to every threat and proposal. In the Orient, there is a belief that the oyster seals itself after catching the first raindrop of April, forever protecting the pearl within. So did Dilber's heart, once touched by Celal Bey, allow no other desire or ambition to penetrate it. No favour, no joy offered by another could ever re-open it.

In this life of wilful and selfless suffering, Dilber yearned for one thing: the peace of a clear conscience, a remedy for all the calamities of her life.

She turned to the woman beside her. 'Your master may have wealth and jewels, but I have a heart. You are asking me to be an odalisque. The very sight of him makes my skin crawl with disgust. I detest him. Go and tell him exactly what I told you!' she said with fervour.

At these words, the woman lost her temper and went straight to her master, telling him that, if such audacity, such rebellion and insolence went unpunished, she would no longer take the responsibility for the slave girls' discipline. Her warning was final. Thus, it was decided that Dilber would be placed in a cell.

Of all the people in the house, it was only Cevher who was infuriated to the point of madness by the master's decision. As they took Dilber to her prison, Cevher stood in the hall and yelled at the top of his voice: 'Does the noble, brave, beautiful tribe of the Caucasus deserve to perish at the hands of African merchants like this?'

They took Dilber to a cold, dark room on the second floor where iron shutters locked out the daylight. Standing there, with a sad smile on her lips, Dilber whispered to herself: 'Behold Cleopatra, imprisoned in a chamber in Egypt'. She affectionately recalled the name that her beloved had mischievously bestowed on her on that day in his drawing room.

In the second night of her imprisonment, Dilber's graceful, strikingly white neck was bent as if weighted down by dark thoughts that haunt the human mind. A few faded memories, shadows under the veil of forgetfulness, paraded before her contemplative eyes. There she was, a young girl, in the thick darkness of the night, searching for her dear mother. Then she recalled her last night in the slave trader's dungeon-like house where she had wrestled with the dark creatures of the night. Her thoughts then drifted to Celal Bey. She could still feel his arm wrapped around her tiny waist and the warmth of that first kiss lingering on her lips. Despite her circumstances and place in society, nature had endowed her with such a tender heart, and now Dilber could feel all the wounds within that heart slowly starting to bleed. For many people, childhood memories, like the golden light of an autumn sun passing over the dried branches of a tree, can breathe life even into an aging face, etched with wrinkles, casting a fleeting touch of youth on it. But for Dilber, it wasn't so. She shut her eyes to keep away the memories of her first mistress, whose violence and fury had caused her profound suffering. She was forced to desert the garden, their first meeting place, her love, her beloved, and she ended up all alone, in a prison cell in Egypt. Who would rescue her from this prison now?

If only she could wake up from this daze and look back. There, she would see her beloved, declaring for the first time: 'You have no idea how much I love you!' She would see his face. A shattered heart, a love affair sold off by cruel hands, a future buried in the past... All this was left behind now. She took out an old photograph from her pocket, its edges worn with her tears, and looked at it with a mix of wonder and longing. Those black eyes, exuding power and determination, that forehead, the seat of his intellect, that countenance expressing both strength and compassion… But it was all gone, all destroyed now.

'This room is dark and cold', she said, looking at the photograph. She placed it on her warm bosom. 'You might get cold here'.

She was thinking… in such piercing silence, in such deep meditation.

All of a sudden, she heard a tapping at the window. First it was soft, then it got louder. She lifted her head up and listened closely. As the noise grew louder, she propped herself up on one arm on the rug and fixed her gaze on the window; her pupils enlarged in fear and horror. What could this noise be, she wondered. It was after midnight. Where could it be coming from? Perhaps it was a thief or a murderer? These could be the final moments of my life, she thought to herself. Dilber was terrified. Her hair was standing on end and her mouth agape, as if separating the chasms of life and death. She was forgotten in this cell, surrounded by many ghosts that refused to leave her alone. But still, she considered it a sanctuary. Who was trying to break the shutters? Who is this iron claw going to stab? Who would it drag from this room to bury in the darkness of the night?

Just as the clamour and commotion of these shapeless nightly creatures that haunt people in times of sorrow and separation began creeping into her mind, threatening to transform her thoughts into doubts that neither education nor experience could dispel, the window shutters burst open and someone entered the room, with blood dripping from wounds on his arms and head. Dilber gasped: 'Who is it?' The intruder, trying to catch his breath, reassured her: 'Don't be afraid. It's me, Cevher! Now… Go down this ladder. Hurry. There's no time to lose!'

'Cevher! It cannot be!' Dilber said.

She walked to Cevher and held his bleeding hand: 'Your goodness, your service to me… It really touches my heart'. She wanted to express her gratitude and debt to him, but Cevher, with a blank stare on his face, said: 'Quick! Hurry! I am bleeding out, and I am starting to feel weak. I've overcome every obstacle to get here. I broke the iron bars. Hurry! Run to your love, to your freedom! Let all of Egypt wake up tomorrow in shock and learn how an impotent slave tore down the iron shutters with his frail arms and saved a beautiful victim of oppression!'

Without saying a word, Dilber approached the open window and started descending. Cevher gripped the ends of the ladder that leaned against the window. He cautioned her: 'Please slow down! The ladder isn't secured and it's already shaking. I know it because I just climbed it. Descend carefully, now. Even more slowly'.

Dilber finally went down with Cevher's help and stood aside, utterly astonished, watching the events unfold in the dark night. Meanwhile, Cevher started to come down, too. The ladder was unsteady, and his legs were shaking, for he was nervous and had lost so much blood. He went down all the way to the fourth step, only to go up again.

'It's too dangerous to come down here', he screamed in fear. When he noticed Dilber reaching out to the base of the ladder to hold it with her tiny hands, Cevher got furious at her for preventing him from fulfilling his sacred wish.

'Get away from there!' he yelled at Dilber. 'Don't you dare throw yourself into any danger! What's the point of holding it from below?' Cevher paused there on the step for a while. He hesitated. Time was ticking away, and the opportunity to save Dilber was fading away. He had climbed up that ladder overcoming a thousand hardships. He had unscrewed the shutters with his bare hands. And now he was hanging on to it by a thread, trying to stabilise the ladder. For a moment, he thought the ladder appeared almost alive, like a treacherous, deceitful creature, a wicked promise of escape. Looking down at the ladder, he yelled: 'You dragon! Leave me be. I will save Dilber!'

But what was the point of lingering up there? He knew that staying there meant ruin, not just for himself, but for Dilber as well. There in this descent lay his ascent toward the ultimate purpose, the hope of Dilber's escape, of saving someone and being saved. He started to go down the steps again; he passed the first rung, then the second. By the third, his legs began to shake, and the ladder started to shake, too. He felt a faint dizziness and hung on to the ladder tightly. Just when he put one foot on the fourth rung, and the other on the fifth, the ladder, like a dragon rearing up, slipped from the window's edge and fell backward with an ominous creak.

Poor Cevher! He lay on the ground, swimming in the unjustly spilled blood of the innocent. Dilber was shaking with shock, grief and horror at this sight. She approached him.

'Ah, you poor Cevher! I have killed you...' she said in anguish. Then she bent down and kissed him on the forehead. Perhaps this affectionate kiss breathed life into his blood-covered body for a quick minute, for Cevher slowly opened his eyes. Dilber cried by his side. 'My dear, merciful Cevher!' she said. 'Ah, why on earth did you do this to yourself? What have I ever done that you sacrificed your life for me?'

Cevher's voice sounded as if it was already resigning to eternal silence. 'Because I love you... But it's all right', he whispered. 'The first time

I looked into your eyes, they had already opened deep wounds in my heart… I would not have survived anyway…'

Dilber held Cevher's head in her arms and kissed his forehead one more time. What a divine, powerful and moving moment this was! Cevher surrendered himself even deeper into her embrace, as if he found comfort giving his last breath under those lips, in those arms. 'I am dying in peace… But you are doomed', he said. 'Ah… Run. Run. Tomorrow… To Istanbul… There is a steamer…' Then, with great effort, he added: 'Your ticket… It's in my pocket'.

Perhaps Cevher had never been happier in his entire life than at that very moment. One could say so from the way in which he buried his Abyssinian-like pale face in Dilber's bosom, and from the way in which he looked at her with his half-opened eyes: his departing soul would much rather nest in Dilber's locks than fly off to heavens. Soon, the horrifying final moment of death invaded Cevher's entire face. Silence! The deep silence of the last few minutes felt as imposing and long as a century. This all-encompassing silence that conquers everything in a veil of mystery, that obliterates the future of humanity into a terrifying abyss beyond the grasp of the human mind and that engulfs the planets in an endless void had now spread its wings over Cevher. Its pitch-black shadow now fell on Cevher's face, like an ominous tombstone covering infinity, as if cast from the darkness of that eternal night.

How was Dilber to return to Istanbul, to the house to which she had once been sold, when she could not even cross a road by herself, uncovered.[1] Her dazzling beauty and eastern propriety stood in the way of such a journey. The mere thought of returning to the merchant's house again! Yes, she knew that all those great doors were shut, making it impossible for her to go back. And yet, she could not even bear the thought of surrendering herself willingly to the merchant, of falling into the arms of lust.

Dilber was shaken to the core, unnerved by the presence of death and nothingness on Cevher's lifeless face, which rested in her arms for some time. She laid his head on the ground and cast one last affectionate glance at him before leaving his side.

As she walked away along the green road lined with date trees, she bowed her head beneath the weight of her thoughts. Moonlight shone through the leaves, casting a sorrowful glow over her long, dishevelled

[1] The emphasis here on being uncovered pertains to Dilber's transition from a private space, the merchant's house, to a public one, highlighting the impossibility of her presence in the public sphere as a woman without her *ferace* or veil, which were not in her possession during her period of confinement.

hair. Moving through the darkness of the night, she looked more like a Greek statue than a real person. The darkness concealed finer details of her gait, yet it boosted her tall posture and demeanour, giving her an imposing presence. As she disappeared into the dark, she looked as if a grieving ancient goddess were walking among the date trees, towards the Nile.

When Dilber reached the Nile, she stopped. It seemed as if she was standing by the river, listening to it sing songs of sorrow and sadness to ancient goddesses. But no! In reality she was neither listening to the churning waters of the river nor thinking about the melancholic, glorious night. For the first time, she lifted her head, hoping to hear a voice, a single sound, that might save her; the same voice that had whispered 'I love you' in her ear a year ago. But alas, just like the last wish of a dying person, this, too, was an impossible one.

Dilber sat by the river, shivering. Exhausted by the pain, she folded her arms across her chest. The Nile's powerful waters, flowing abundantly at that time of the year, touched her toes. She looked around. Perhaps she had a secret to impart, or a last word to entrust, but to whom could she tell it? The river is merciless! The trees, cold-hearted! And the moon, trying to escape from among the clouds, indifferent!

As her soul ascended to the heavens, her body sank deeper into the waters of the Nile.

Like a sudden flash of light, the cold, fatal whirls of the Nile sucked Dilber into its depths a few times before finally releasing her. On its surface, she looked as pure as the eastern sky and as pure as love itself. Dilber was caught in the current, drifting on the surface of the river. Her long hair danced on the water, and the moonlight glimmered on her pale face, a face that was now devoid of every expression of desire, hope and wish. The only colour left on her face was the lifeless hue of the ever-more melancholic moon. All her sorrows and suffering had ebbed away; all the love and dreams had faded.

One wonders… where are these horrific whirls, these deadly currents of the Nile taking this poor Dilber, this unfortunate slave?

To her freedom!

Appendix A: Slave Sale Deed #1

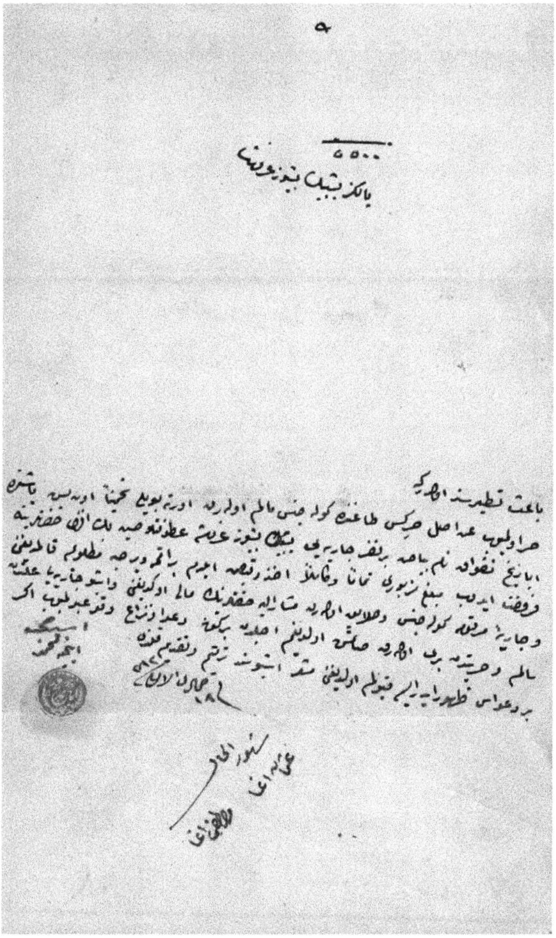

Appendix A Courtesy of IBB Atatürk Library.

Slave Sale Deed #1 English Translation[1]

5,500

Only five thousand five hundred *kuruş*.

The reason for writing this deed is:
I hereby sell a slave girl I owned, coming from a slave lineage and from the Circassian mountains, built of medium height, approximately fifteen years old, white *cariye*, by the name Abazıh Nakvan, to the honourable Hüseyin Bey, and I received a total sum of 5,500 *kuruş* in full. I hereby attest that not a single penny remains due and the *cariye* of a slave status named in this deed now is the property of the afore-mentioned master.

This slave is handed over free of illness and with no claim to freedom. For this reason, should any dispute or claim arise regarding her status, I hereby declare with this deed that I accept full responsibility.

Dated: 18 Jumada al-Awwal, year 1282 (22 September 1865).

Signed:
Slave Trader İnce Mehmed
[Mehmed Emin]

Witnesses:
Osman Agha
Mustafa Agha
Three individuals.

Deeds of sale for the purchased white *cariyes*.
Dated: 18 Jumada al-Awwal, year 1282.

[1] *5500. Yalnız beş bin beş yüz guruş. Bâ*ᶜ*is-i tastîr-i sened oldur ki: Hür olmayub* ᶜ*an-asl Çerkes dağında köle cins mâlım olarak orta boylu tahmînen on beş yaşında Abazıh Nakvan nâm beyâz bir nefer câriyeyi beş bin beş yüz guruşa* ᶜ*atûfetlü Hüseyin Bey efendi hazretlerine furuht idüb meblağ-ı mezbûru tamâmen ve kâmilen ahz û kabz eyledim bir akçe ve bir habbe matlûbum kalmadığını ve câriye-yi merkûme köle cins ve halâyık olarak müşârun ileyh hazretlerinin mâlı olduğunu ve işbu câriyeyi* ᶜ*illetden sâlim ve hürriyetten berî olarak satmış olduğum ecilden bir gûne da*ᶜ*vâ ve nizâ*ᶜ *vukû*ᶜ *bulmayub eğer bir da*ᶜ*vâsı zuhûr iderse kabûlüm olduğunu müş*ᶜ*ir işbu sened terkîm ve takdîm kılındı. Fî 18 Cemâziye'l-ûlâ sene 282. Esîrci İnce Mehmed. [Mehmed Emin]. Şühûd-ül hâl.* ᶜ*Osmân Ağa. Mustafa Ağa. Üç nefer. Mübâya*ᶜ*a olunan beyâz câriyelerin senedleri. Fî 18 Ca sene 282*

Appendix B: Slave Sale Deed #2

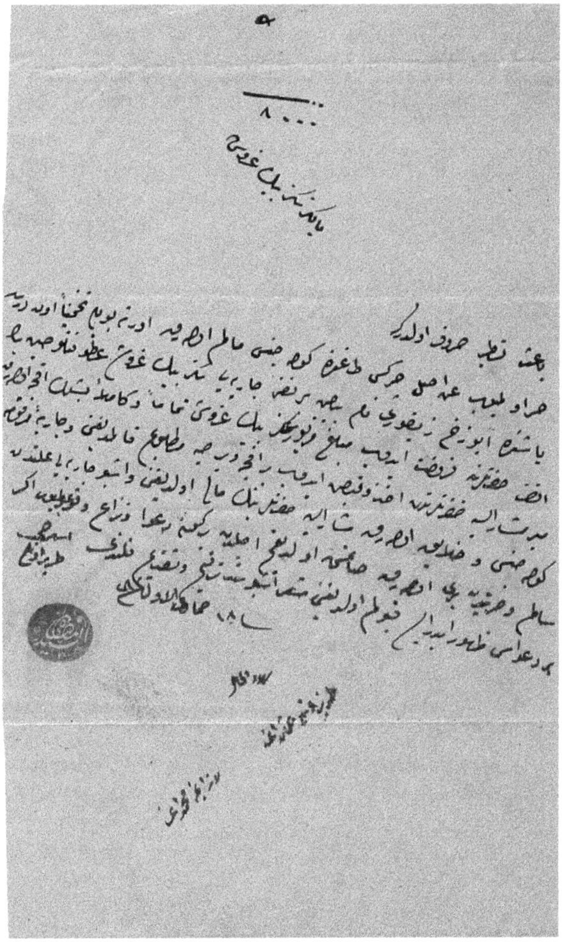

Appendix B Courtesy of IBB Atatürk Library.

Slave Sale Deed #2 English Translation[1]

8,000

Only eight thousand *kuruş*.

The reason for writing this deed is as follows:
I hereby sell a slave girl I owned, coming from a slave lineage and from the Circassian mountains, built of medium height, approximately fourteen years old, white *cariye*, by the name Obuzih Zikuri, to the honourable Hüseyin Bey for the amount of eight thousand *kuruş* in five-*akçe* coins. I hereby attest that not a single penny remains due and the *cariye* of a slave status named in this deed now is the property of the afore-mentioned master. This slave is handed over free of illness and with no claim to freedom. For this reason, should any dispute or claim arise regarding her status, I hereby declare with this deed that I accept full responsibility.

Dated: 18 Jumada al-Awwal, year 1282 (22 September 1865).

Signed:
Esirci (Slave Trader) from Trabzon
[The Honourable Seyyid Mustafa]

Witnesses:
Trabzonlu Osman Agha
Laz İnce Mehmed Agha

[1] *8000 Yalnız sekiz bin guruş*
Bâ^{c}is-i tastîr-i hurûf oldur ki
Hür olmayub ^{c}an-asl Çerkes dağında köle cins mâlım olarak orta boylu tahmînen on dört yaşında Obuzih Zikuri nâm beyâz bir nefer câriyeyi sekiz bin guruşa ^{c}atûfetlü Hüseyin Bey efendi hazretlerine furuht idüb meblağ-ı mezbûr sekiz bin guruşu tamâmen ve kâmilen beşlik akçe olarak mîr-i müşârün ileyh hazretlerinden ahz û kabz idüb bir akçe ve bir habbe matlûbum kalmadığını ve câriye-yi merkûme köle cins ve halâyık olarak müşârun ileyh hazretlerinin mâlı olduğunu ve işbu câriyeyi ^{c}illetden sâlim ve hürriyetden berî olarak satmış olduğum ecilden bir gûne da^{c}vâ ve nizâ^{c} vukû^{c} bulmayub eğer bir da^{c}vâsı zuhûr iderse kabûlüm olduğunu müş^{c}ir işbu sened terkîm ve takdîm kılındı
Fî 18 Cemâziye'l-ûlâ sene 282
Esîrci Trabzonlu [Es-seyyid Mustafa]
Şühûd-ül hâl
Trabzonlu ^{c}Osmân Ağa
Laz İnce Mehmed Ağa

Appendix C: Slave Sale Deed #3

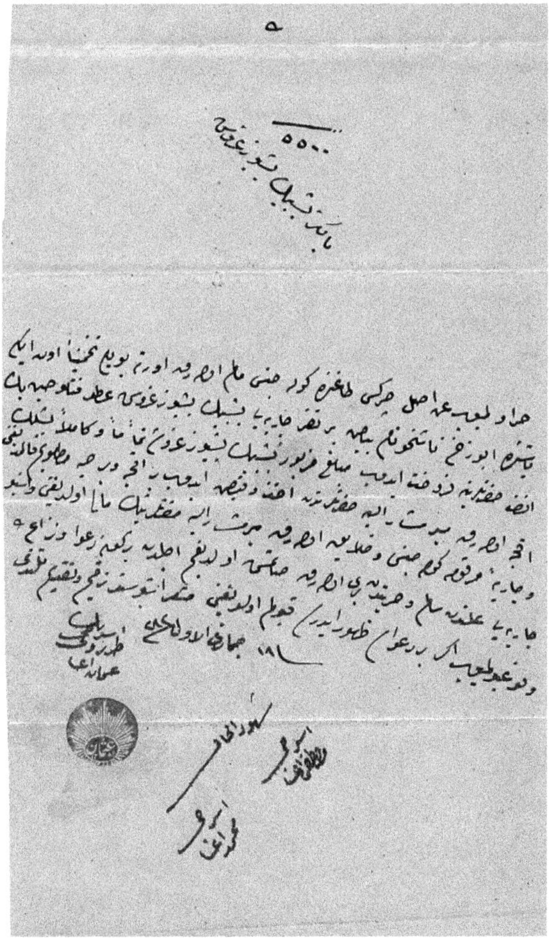

Appendix C Courtesy of IBB Atatürk Library.

Slave Sale Deed #3 English Translation[1]

5,500

Only five thousand five hundred *kuruş*.

The reason for writing this deed is as follows:
I hereby sell a slave girl I owned, coming from a slave lineage and from the Circassian mountains, built of medium height, approximately twelve years old, white *cariye*, by the name Obuzih Naşhu, to the honourable Hüseyin Bey for the amount of eight thousand *kuruş* in five-*akçe* coins. I hereby attest that not a single penny remains due and the *cariye* of a slave status named in this deed now is the property of the afore-mentioned master.

This slave is handed over free of illness and with no claim to freedom. For this reason, should any dispute or claim arise regarding her status, I hereby declare with this deed that I accept full responsibility.

Dated: 18 Jumada al-Awwal, year 1282 (22 September 1865).

Signed:
Slave Trader from Trabzon
[Osman Agha]

Witnesses:
Slave Trader Mustafa Agha
Slave Trader Mehmed Agha

[1] *5500 Yalnız beş bin beş yüz guruş*
Bâ^{c}is-i tastîr-i sened oldur ki
Hür olmayub ^{c}an-asl Çerkes dağında köle cins mâlım olarak orta boylu tahmînen on iki yaşında Obuzih Naşhu nâm beyâz bir nefer câriyeyi beş bin beş yüz guruşa ^{c}atûfetlü Hüseyin Bey efendi hazretlerine furuht idüb meblağ-ı mezbûr beş bin beş yüz guruşu tamâmen ve kâmilen beşlik akçe olarak mîr-i müşârün ileyh hazretlerinden ahz û kabz idüb bir akçe ve bir habbe matlûbum kalmadığını ve câriye-yi merkûme köle cins ve halâyık olarak mîr-i müşârun ileyh hazretlerinin mâlı olduğunu ve işbu câriyeyi ^{c}illetden sâlim ve hürriyetden berî olarak satmış olduğum ecilden bir gûne da^{c}vâ ve nizâ^{c} vukû^{c} bulmayub eğer bir da^{c}vâsı zuhûr iderse kabûlüm olduğunu müş^{c}ir işbu sened terkîm ve takdîm kılındı
Fî 18 Cemâziye'l-ûlâ sene 282
Bende
Esîrci Trabzonlu ^{c}Osmân Ağa
[^{c}Osmân]
Şühûd-ül hâl
Esîrci Mustafa Ağa
Esîrci Mehmed Ağa

Appendix D: Slave Sale Deed #4

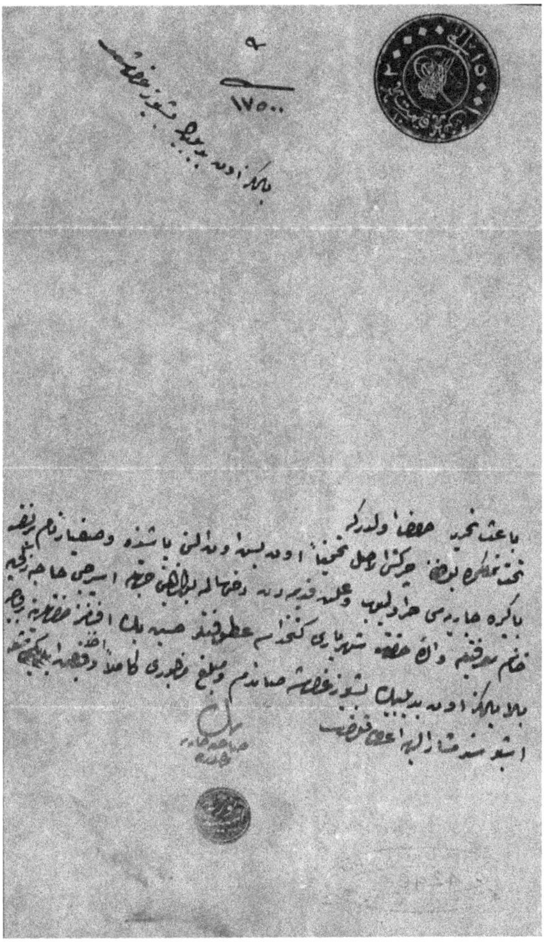

Appendix D Courtesy of IBB Atatürk Library.

Slave Sale Deed #4 English Translation[1]

17,500

Only seventeen thousand five hundred *kuruş*.

The reason for writing this deed is as follows:
I hereby sell a virgin slave girl under my possession, named Vasfıyar, of Circassian origins, free of illness and with no claim to freedom, approximately fifteen or sixteen years of age, to the honourable Hüseyin Bey, the steward to Her Majesty the Sultan's Mother, by the mediation of the slave trader Hâce Zekiye Hanım, for the amount of seventeen thousand and five hundred *kuruş*, as stated above. I hereby declare with this deed that I have received the full amount.

Signed: Owner of the afore-mentioned *cariye*
[Emine Nuriye]

The deed of sale for the purchased white *cariye*.

[1] *[Min 1500 ilâ 2000 kıymet]*
17500 Yalnız on yedi bin beş yüz guruş
Bâ^c is-i tahrîr i hurûf oldur ki
Taht-ı temellükümde bulunan
Çerkes ül-asl tahmînen on beş on altı yaşında Vasfıyar nâm bir nefer bâkire câriyemi hür olmayub ve ^c illet-i kadîmeden dahi sâlime bulunduğu cihetle esîrci Hâce Zekiye Hânım ma^c rifetiyle vâlide-yi hazret-i şehriyârî kethüdâsı ^c atûfetlü Hüseyin Bey hazretlerine bervech-i bâlâ yalnız on yedi bin beş yüz guruşa satdım ve meblağ-ı mezkûru kâmilen azh û kabz eylediğimi müş^c ir işbu sened müşârun ileyhe i^c tâ kılındı.
Bende
Sâhibe-yi câriye-yi mezkûre
[Emîne Nûriye]
Mübâya^c a olunan beyaz câriyenin senedi

Appendix E: Slave Sale Deed #5

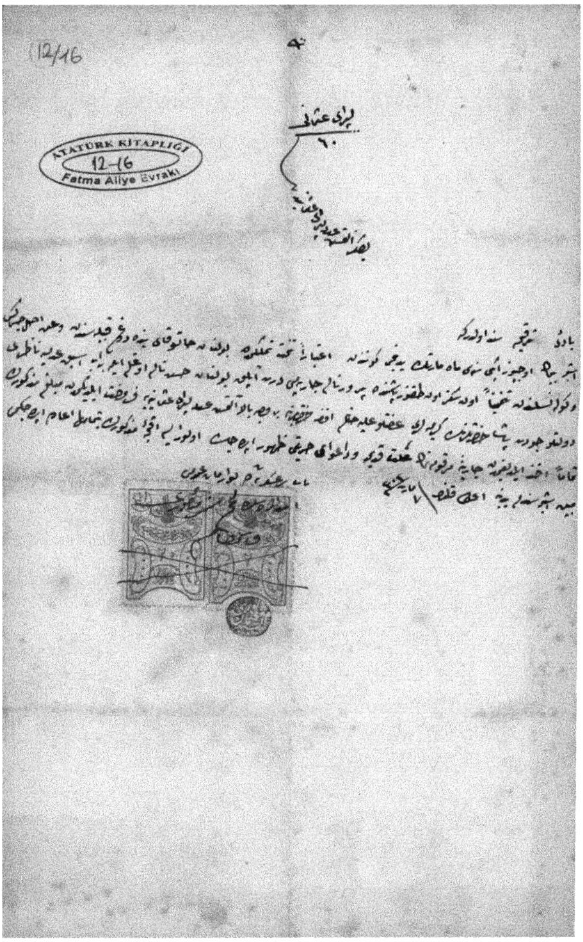

Appendix E Courtesy of IBB Atatürk Library.

Slave Sale Deed #5 English Translation[1]

Ottoman Lira: 60

Only Sixty Ottoman lira

The reason for writing this deed is as follows:
On the seventh day of the month of March in the year 1302, I hereby sell the slave girl named Perver, aged approximately eighteen or nineteen, from the Hatukay Bjeduğ tribe and of Circassian origin and of slave descent, who has previously been under my possession, together with her son named Hasan, aged four months, to the esteemed Aliye Hanım, daughter of the former Minister of Justice, the venerable Cevdet Pasha, for the amount of sixty Ottoman liras, as stated above. Having fully received the afore-mentioned amount, I further declare that, should any pre-existing illness or a claim for her freedom arise regarding the afore-mentioned slave girl, I will return the entire sum received. This document is therefore issued as proof.

Dated: 7 March, year 1302 [19 March 1886]

General Provisions at the Office of the Seraskerate
Head Clerk:
Provincial Governor: [The Honourable Seyyid Osman Nuri]

[1] *Lîrâ-yı ᶜOsmânî*
60 Yalnız altmış ᶜaded Lîrâ-yı
ᶜOsmânîdir
Bâᶜis-i terkîm-i sened oldur ki
İşbu bin üç yüz iki senesi mâh-ı Martın yedinci gününden iᶜtibâren taht-ı temellükümde bulunan Hatukay Bjeduğ kabîlesinden ve ᶜan-asl Çerkes ve köle neslinden ve tahmînen on sekiz on dokuz yaşında Perver nâm câriyeyi dört aylık bulunan Hasan nâm oğlu ile berâber esbak ᶜAdliye Nâzırı devletlü Cevdet Paşa hazretlerinin kerîmeleri ᶜatûfetlü ᶜAliye Hânım efendi hazretlerine bervech-i bâlâ altmış ᶜaded Lîrâ-yı ᶜOsmâniyeye furuht eylediğimden meblağ-ı mezkûrun tamâmen ahz eylediğimden câriye-yi merkûmenin ᶜillet-i kadîme ve daᶜvâ-yı hürriyeti zuhûr edecek olur ise akçe-yi mezkûrun tamâmını iᶜâde edeceğimi mübeyyin işbu senedim yedine iᶜtâ kılındı.
fî 7 Mart sene 302
*Bâb-ı Serᶜaskerîde Levâzımât-ı ᶜUmûmî *** *** Serme˒mûru Kâ˒immakâmı*
[Es-seyyid ᶜOsmân Nûrî]

Chronology

Year	Political History	History of Ottoman Slavery	History of Ottoman Literature	Sezai's Biography
1839	The Edict of Gülhane, issued by Sultan Abdülmecid I, marks the beginning of the Tanzimat (Reform) era.			
1846		Closure of the Istanbul Slave Market by order of Abdülmecid I.		
1847		Suppression of the slave trade in the Persian Gulf, as the British secure Ottoman cooperation.		
1851			First Ottoman novel, Hovsep Vartanyan's *Akabi Hikayesi* (The Story of Akabi) is published in Armeno-Turkish, paving the way for Ottoman novelistic traditions.	
1854		Abdülmecid I issues a *firman* prohibiting the slave trade of Circassians and Georgians, under pressure from Britain and France.		
1855		Prohibition of sale of African slaves to Crete and Jannina, blocking a key transit point.		

1857		General prohibition of the black slave trade across the Ottoman Empire.		
1859				Samipaşazade Sezai is born as the son of Abdurrahman Sami Pasha, the first Ottoman Minister of Education, and Gülarayiş Hanım, a slave from the Caucasus.
1859–64	Following Russia's conquest of the Caucasus, hundreds of thousands of Circassians flee as refugees to the Ottoman Empire, and many are sold into slavery.			
1860			First translations from European literature appear in Ottoman Turkish, followed by original Ottoman works in the 1870s by intellectuals and early Tanzimat writers, including Şinasi, Namık Kemal and Ahmet Mithat.	
1861	Abdülaziz ascends to the throne after the death of his brother, Abdülmecid I.			

Year	Political History	History of Ottoman Slavery	History of Ottoman Literature	Sezai's Biography
1876	After his brother Abdülaziz's deposition, Abdülhamid II ascends to the throne and promulgates the First Constitution, initiating the First Constitutional Era (1876–78). However, he quickly suspends it, ruling as an absolute monarch for the next three decades.			
1877		Reaffirmation of the 1857 general prohibition on the trade of African slaves.		At seventeen, Sezai meets his idol, Namık Kemal, in Sultanahmet Prison, where his frequent visits forge a friendship that will shape his literary and ideological growth.
1879				Sezai starts working for the Imperial Correspondence Office.
1880		Anglo-Ottoman convention for the suppression of trade in African slaves.		
1881–85				Sezai serves as clerk at the Ottoman Embassy in London, gaining further exposure to European art

1885			After his dismissal from the London post, Sezai stays in Paris, where he marries Latife Hanım, daughter of the Tunisian Mahmud b. Ayat, though the marriage is brief. In Paris, Sezai immerses himself in opera and theatre. He is appointed as clerk to the Vienna Embassy but declines the position.
1886			Return to Istanbul. His mother Gülarayiş Hanım dies. Sezai begins work as advisor in the Ottoman Foreign Ministry, a position he holds until 1901. His major works are products of these *istibdad* years under Abdülhamid II's autocratic rule.
1888		Sezai's *Adventures of a Slave Girl* is published.	Vuslat, Sezai's first love, a Circassian slave he knew from his father's mansion, dies.

Year	Political History	History of Ottoman Slavery	History of Ottoman Literature	Sezai's Biography
1889		Ottoman law against African slave trade.		
1890		General act of the Brussels Conference to suppress African slave trade, with the Ottoman Empire signing on to anti-slavery measures.		
1891			*Küçük Şeyler* (Little Things), Sezai's short-story collection, is published, becoming a cornerstone of Ottoman realism.	
1896			The journal *Servet-i Fünun* becomes the leading platform for the *Edebiyat-ı Cedide* (New Literature) movement under the editorship of Tevfik Fikret. Introducing modernist prose and poetry influenced by French literature, it brings together key figures such as Halit Ziya Uşaklıgil, Mehmet Rauf and Hüseyin Cahit Yalçın, all influenced by Sezai's realist writing.	
1898			Sezai's *Rumûzü'l-Edeb*, a collection of essays on literary aesthetics and criticism, is published.	

1901			*Servet-i Fünun* is shut down by Hamidian censorship, marking the end of the *Edebiyat-ı Cedide* movement.	Sezai goes into voluntary exile in Paris, joins the Young Turks and publishes political pieces critical of the Hamidian regime in *Şûrâ-yı Ümmet*, the Committee of Union and Progress (CUP)'s publication.
1908	The Second Constitution is proclaimed as the Committee of Union and Progress (CUP) forces Sultan Abdülhamid II to restore the constitution.	The Ottoman Ministry of Justice conveys a notice to the Ministry of Interior to start deliberation on the abolition of trade in Circassian slaves, with partial results.		With the proclamation of the Second Constitution, Sezai returns first to Salonika, then to Istanbul.
1909	After the 31 March Incident, Abdülhamid II is deposed by the CUP and exiled to Salonika.	After Abdülhamid II's deposition, the CUP issues telegrams to Circassian settlements, informing families to reclaim their relatives, leading to the emancipation of 213 female slaves from the Yıldız Palace. However, this move does not extend to the household slaves of notable statesmen, leaving the broader system of domestic slavery intact.		Sezai is appointed as Ottoman Ambassador to Madrid, representing the empire in Spain.

Year	Political History	History of Ottoman Slavery	History of Ottoman Literature	Sezai's Biography
1914–18	World War I. The Ottoman Empire joins the Central Powers, facing military defeat and internal strife.			From 1916 to the end of the war, Sezai lives in Switzerland, where he resumes his literary work, contributing a series of essays titled 'Swiss Memoirs' to the newspaper *İkdam*.
1918–23	Following World War I, Istanbul and key Ottoman territories are occupied by Allied forces under the Armistice of Mudros, triggering political turmoil and resistance that culminates in the Turkish War of Independence. Starting in 1919, the Turkish War of Independence led by Mustafa Kemal resists Allied occupation.			
1920	The Turkish Grand National Assembly (TBMM) is established in Ankara, marking the foundation of a new government independent of the Ottoman Sultanate.			

1921				Removed from his post in Spain, Sezai returns to Istanbul and devotes himself to writing.
1922	The Ottoman Sultanate is abolished, officially ending Ottoman rule.			
1923	The Turkish Grand National Assembly declares Turkey a republic and elects Mustafa Kemal as its first president, officially establishing the Republic of Turkey. Turkey signs the Treaty of Lausanne, securing the international recognition of its sovereignty and modern borders.			
1924	The caliphate is abolished, marking the separation of religion and state.			Second edition of *The Adventures of a Slave Girl* is published, with minor revisions and a new preface by Sezai.

Year	Political History	History of Ottoman Slavery	History of Ottoman Literature	Sezai's Biography
1926		The Convention to Suppress the Slave Trade and Slavery (1926 Slavery Convention) is issued by the League of Nations and signed by member states. Turkey, not yet a member, joins the League in 1932 but does not sign the treaty at that time.		
1927				The Grand Assembly grants Sezai a pension, and Istanbul Municipality provides him with a house in Kadıköy.
1933		Slavery abolished in Turkey. Following its 1932 membership in the League of Nations, Turkey enacts legal reforms aligning with international conventions, officially ending slavery.		
1937				Sezai passes away and is buried in Küçüksu Cemetery in Istanbul.

Further Reading on Ottoman Slavery

Ali, Kecia. *Marriage and Slavery in Early Islam*. Harvard University Press, 2010.

Beach, Adam R. 'Lady Mary Wortley Montagu and Slavery in the Ottoman (and the British) Empire'. *Philological Quarterly*, vol. 85, no. 3–4, June 2006, pp. 293–314.

Camoglu, Arif. 'The Novel and the Ottoman Institution of Slavery: Domesticity and Slave Labor in Namık Kemal's *İntibah*'. *Novel: A Forum on Fiction*, vol. 57, no. 2, Aug. 2024, pp. 145–61.

Canbakal, Hülya, and Alpay Filiztekin. 'Slavery and Decline of Slave-Ownership in Ottoman Bursa, 1460–1880'. *International Labor and Working-Class History*, vol. 97, 2020, pp. 57–80.

Cuno, Kenneth, and Terence Waltz. *Race and Slavery in the Middle East: Histories of Trans-Saharan Africans in Nineteenth-Century Egypt, Sudan, and the Ottoman Mediterranean*. The American University of Cairo Press, 2010.

Erdem, Yusuf Hakan. 'Tanzimat Döneminde Kölelik, 1846–1876'. *Tanzimat: Değişim Sürecinde Osmanlı İmparatorluğu*, edited by Halil İnalcık and Mehmet Seyitdanlıoğlu, Türkiye İş Bankası, 2011, pp. 625–63.

———. (2010). 'Magic, Theft, and Arson: The Life and Death of an Enslaved African Woman in Ottoman İzmit'. *Race and Slavery in The Middle East: Histories of Trans-Saharan Africans in Nineteenth-Century Egypt, Sudan, and the Ottoman Mediterranean*, edited by Terence Walz and Kenneth Cuno, American University of Cairo Press, 2010, pp. 125–46.

———. *Slavery in the Ottoman Empire and Its Demise, 1800–1909*. Palgrave Macmillan, 1996.

Ferguson, Michael. 'Abolitionism and the African Slave Trade in the Ottoman Empire (1857–1922)'. *The Palgrave Handbook of Bondage and Human Rights in Africa and Asia*, edited by Alessandro Stanziani and Gwyn Campbell, Palgrave Macmillan, 2020, pp. 209–26.

———. 'Clientship, Social Indebtedness, and State-Controlled Emancipation of Africans in the Late Ottoman Empire'. *Debt and Slavery in the Mediterranean and Atlantic Worlds*, edited by Gwyn Campbell and Alessandro Stanziani, Taylor & Francis, 2015, pp. 49–62.

Foster, William. *Gender, Mastery and Slavery: From European to Atlantic World Frontiers*. Bloomsbury Publishing, 2009.

Gürsel, Burcu. 'Dissolving into the Nile: Ottoman Reformism and Maternal Slavery in *Sergüzeşt*'. *Narratives of Dislocation in the Arab World: Rewriting Ghurba*, edited by Nadeen Dakkak. Routledge, 2023, pp. 25–46.

Hain, Kathryn A., and Matthew Gordon. *Concubines and Courtesans: Women and Slavery in Islamic History*. Oxford University Press, 2017.

Karamürsel, Ceyda. 'Relics of an Unwanted Past: Slavery, Polygamy and the Harem at the End of the Ottoman Empire'. *Gender and History*, vol. 37, no. 2, 2023, pp. 653–66.

———. 'Transplanted Slavery, Contested Freedom, and Vernacularization of Rights in the Reform Era Ottoman Empire'. *Comparative Studies in Society and History*, vol. 59, no. 3, 2017, pp. 690–714.

———. 'The Uncertainties of Freedom: The Second Constitutional Era and the End of Slavery in the Late Ottoman Empire'. *Journal of Women's History*, vol. 28, no. 3, 2016, pp. 138–61.

Lewis, Bernard. *Race and Slavery in the Middle East: An Historical Enquiry*. Oxford University Press, 1990.

Mowafi, Reda. *Slavery, Slave Trade, and Abolition Attempts in Egypt and the Sudan, 1820–1882*. Esselte Studium, 1981.

Manning, Peter. *Slave Trades, 1500–1800: Globalization of Forced Labour*. Taylor & Francis, 2016.

Özdemir, Özgül. 'A Slave between Empires: A Transimperial History of North Africa, by M'hamed Oualdi'. *Journal of Global Slavery*, vol. 5, no. 3, 2020, pp. 407–10.

Powell, Eve Troutt. *Tell This in My Memory: Stories of Enslavement from Egypt, Sudan, and the Ottoman Empire*. Stanford University Press, 2012.

Roberts, Mary. *Intimate Outsiders: The Harem in Ottoman and Orientalist Art and Travel Literature*. Duke University Press, 2007.

Roşu, Felicia. *Slavery in the Black Sea Region, c. 900–1900: Forms of Unfreedom at the Intersection between Christianity and Islam*. Brill, 2021.

Segal, Ronald. *Islam's Black Slaves: The Other Black Diaspora*. Farrar, Straus and Giroux, 2002.

Sezai, Samipaşazade. *Dilber, esclave, et l'eunuque amoureux*. Translated by Besim Ömer Pasha, Société anonyme turque d'imprimerie et de publication, 1933.

Toledano, Ehud R. *As if Silent and Absent: Bonds of Enslavement in the Islamic Middle East*. Yale University Press, 2007.

———. *Slavery and Abolition in the Ottoman Middle East*. University of Washington Press, 2012.

———. 'Abolition and Anti-Slavery in the Ottoman Empire: A Case to Answer?' *A Global History of Anti-Slavery Politics in the Nineteenth Century*, edited by W. Mulligan and M. Bric, Palgrave Macmillan, 2013, pp. 117–36.

———. *The Ottoman Slave Trade and Its Suppression: 1840–1890*. Princeton University Press, 2014.

———. 'Late Ottoman Concepts of Slavery'. *Poetics Today*, vol. 14, no. 3, 1993, pp. 477–506.

Zilfi, Madeline. *Women and Slavery in the Late Ottoman Empire: The Design of Difference*. Cambridge University Press, 2012.